LUCRETIUS:

DE RERUM NATURA IV

D1719313

edited with translation and commentary by

John Godwin

ARIS & PHILLIPS

2nd. corrected impression 1992.

Lucretius Carus, Titus
  [De rerum natura. Book 4. *English & Latin*]
  De rerum natura IV. — (Classical texts)
  I. [De rerum natura. Book 4. *English & Latin*]
  II. Title   III. Godwin, J.   IV. Series
  871'.01   PA6483.E5

ISBN 0 85668 308 6 *cloth*
ISBN 0 85668 309 4 *limp*

Printed and published in England by ARIS & PHILLIPS LTD.
Teddington House, Church Street, Warminster, Wiltshire, England.

CONTENTS

To my parents – with love and gratitude

PREFACE

'Lucretius speaks across the years to the modern reader more directly, and enlists his interest more immediately, than almost any other poet of antiquity.' (D.E.W. Wormell, 'The Personal World of Lucretius' in *Lucretius* ed Dudley) The *De Rerum Natura* is the great epic of Man and the Universe, a *tour de force* of literary genius and a window into a world as familiar to us as it was to the Romans of the 1st century B.C. Nature – and human nature – have not changed; consequently the impact of Lucretius' ideas – concerning perennial questions of philosophy and charged with a directness and practicality that is unique – has not been eroded with the passage of time, but strikes us today with all the personal authenticity of a man speaking to men. The fourth book in particular is of enormous interest both literary – the famous diatribe on Romantic Love is indispensable reading for anyone interested in Love poetry – philosophical, scientific, and simply human, as we watch an intellectual giant attempting to come to terms with reality as we perceive it through the normal everyday spectacle of life.

Yet the fourth book of the *De Rerum Natura* has never been edited in English separately from the rest of the poem. It is the purpose of this edition to make the work accessible to everybody – in particular those who are picking up Lucretius for the first time. The translation is primarily functional rather than aesthetic – designed to elucidate rather than to rival the original – but will enable those without Latin to derive some idea of the meaning and significance of this poem. The Introduction and Commentary presuppose no knowledge of Latin except in the elucidation of certain linguistic and textual matters. The commentary makes no claim to be exhaustive – but where corners have been cut I have tried to indicate where further information may be found.

My debts to other scholars are of course enormous. Nobody can edit Lucretius without to a large extent being guided and informed by the great editions of Munro, Ernout-Robin and Bailey – if I had acknowledged every single point owed to them the book would be twice the length.

Similarly, the work of Jonathan Barnes in philosophy and David West in literary criticism have been of constant help and inspiration in the preparation of this book. My thanks go also to Mr C.D.N. Costa, who read a large part of the commentary in draft form and saved me from myself on many points, and to Mr John Aris, to whose enterprise and enthusiasm this book owes its existence.

John Godwin
Shrewsbury December 1985

BIBLIOGRAPHY AND ABBREVIATIONS

Abbreviations appear in brackets

Works of Reference

The Oxford Classical Dictionary (2nd Edition, Oxford 1970) (*OCD²*)
The Oxford Latin Dictionary (Oxford 1982) (*OLD*)

Texts

The most accessible text of Epicurus is to be found in Diogenes Laertius *Lives of Eminent Philosophers* vol. 2 (London-Cambridge, Mass., 1925) Loeb Classical Library; with facing English translation. The most complete text of Epicurus is in Arrighetti: *Epicuro, Opere* (2nd edition, Torino 1973), with Italian translation and notes. For the texts of the Presocratic Philosophers, see: Kirk, Raven and Schofield: *The Presocratic Philosophers* (2nd edition, Cambridge 1983), with English translation and full discussion. Fragments not contained there will be found in: H.Diels *Die Fragmente der Vorsokratiker* (6th edition, revised W. Kranz, Berlin 1952) (D-K). The two surviving works of Sextus Empiricus, *Outlines of Pyrrhonism* (OP) and *Against the Mathematicians* (AM) are available in the Loeb Classical Library (Greek text with facing English translation) edited by R.G. Bury (4 vols. 1933-47).

Editions of Lucretius referred to:

Editio Aldina (Avancius) Venice 1500
Editio Juntina (Candidus) Firenze, 1512.
Lambinus, D. (Paris, 1563-4, 1565, 1570; Frankfurt, 1583)
Lachmann, K. (Berlin 1850)
Munro, H.A.J. (Cambridge, 1864, 1866, 1873, 1886)
Giussani, C. (Torino 1896-8)
Bailey, C. (Oxford, 1900, 1922) (OCT)
Ernout-Robin (second edition, Paris 1962)
Martin, J. (Leipzig, 5th edition 1963)
Leonard-Smith (Madison 1942)
Bailey, C. (3 vols. Oxford, 1947)

Smith, M.F. (Loeb Classical Library, 1975)
Müller, K. (Zurich, 1975)

Editions of single books of the *DRN*

Book 1, edited by P. Michael Brown (Bristol, 1984)
Book 3, edited by E.J. Kenney (Cambridge, 1971)
Book 5, edited by C.D.N. Costa (Oxford, 1985)

Other works cited:

Adams, J.N., *The Latin Sexual Vocabulary* (Duckworth 1982).
Amory, A., '*Obscura de re lucida carmina*: Science and poetry
        in *De Rerum Natura*', *Yale Classical Studies* 21 (1969)
        143-68.
Annas, J. and Barnes, J., *The Modes of Scepticism* (Cambridge
        1985).
Arragon, R.F., 'Poetic art as a Philosophic Medium for Lucretius'
        Essays in Criticism 11 (1961) 371-89.
Asmis, E., 'Lucretius' Explanation of Moving Dream Figures at
        4.768-76', *American Journal of Philology* 102 (1981) 138-45.
Bailey, C., *The Greek Atomists and Epicurus* (Oxford, 1928).
Barigazzi, A., 'Epicure et le Scepticisme' *Association Guillaume
        Budé:Actes de Congres* (1969) 286-93.
Barnes, J., *The Presocratic Philosophers* (2nd ed. London 1982).
Barnes, Brunschwig, Burnyeat and Schofield (edd), *Science
        and Speculation* (Cambridge, 1982) .
Barone, C., 'Le spese e le illusioni degli amanti (L.4.1123-30)'
        Studi Urbinati di Storia, Filosofia e Letterature 52 (1978)
        75-90.
Bergson, H., *The Philosophy of Poetry:the Genius of Lucretius*
        (New York, 1959).
Betensky, A., 'Lucretius and Love' *Classical World* 73 (1980)
        291-9.
Boyancé, P., *Lucrèce et l'Epicurisme* (Paris 1963).
Bright, D.F., 'The Plague and the structure of *De Rerum Natura*'
        Latomus 30 (1971) 607-32.
Brown, R.D., 'Lucretius and Callimachus' *Illinois Classical
        Studies* 7 (1982) 77-97.
    —   'Lucretian Ridicule of Anaxagoras' *Classical
        Quarterly* 33 (1983) 146-60.
Burnyeat, M.F., 'The Upside-down Back-to-Front Sceptic of
        Lucretius 4.472' *Philologus* 122 (1978) 197-206.
Canfora, L., 'I Proemi del *De Rerum Natura*' *Rivista di Filologia
        e di Istruzione Classica* 110 (1982) 63-77.

Carcopino, J., *Daily Life in Ancient Rome* (Harmondsworth 1956).

Clarke, M.L., 'Lucretius 4.1026' *Classical Quarterly* 34 (1984) 240.

Classen, C.J., 'Poetry and Rhetoric in Lucretius' *Transactions of the American Philological Association* 99 (1968) 77–118.

Clausen, W., 'Callimachus and Roman Poetry' *Greek, Roman and Byzantine Studies* 5 (1964) 181–96.

    — 'Two Conjectures' *American Journal of Philology* 84 (1963) 415–7.

Clay, D., 'The Sources of Lucretius' Inspiration' *Études sur l'Epicurisme Antique* (*Cahiers de Philologie* 1 (1976)) 205–27.

Commager, H.S., 'Lucretius' Interpretation of the Plague' *Harvard Studies in Classical Philology* 62 (1957) 105–21.

Commager, S., *The Odes of Horace* (Indiana 1962).

Copley, F.O., *Exclusus Amator* (American Philological Association Monograph 17, Baltimore 1956).

Cox, A., 'Didactic Poetry' in (ed.) J. Higginbotham, *Greek and Latin Literature, a Comparative Study* (London 1969) 124–61.

Cox, A.S., 'Lucretius and his Message: a Study in the Prologues of the *De Rerum Natura*' *Greece and Rome* 18 (1971) 1–16.

Dalzell, A., 'Some Recent Work on the Text of Lucretius' *Phoenix* 14 (1960) 96–105.

Dodds, E.R., *The Greeks and the Irrational* (California 1951).

Dudley, D.R., (ed), *Lucretius* (London 1965).

Ferrero, L., *Poetica Nuova in Lucrezio* (Florence 1949).

Fitzgerald, W., 'Lucretius' Cure for Love in the *De Rerum Natura*' *Classical World* 78 (1984) 73–86.

Frazer, J.G., *The Golden Bough* (London 1911).

Fraenkel, E., *Horace* (Oxford 1957).

Friedländer, L., *Roman Life and Manners* (London 1907).

Furley, D.J., 'Lucretius and the Stoics' *Bulletin of the Institute of Classical Studies* 13 (1966) 13–33.

    Two Studies in the Greek Atomists (Princeton 1967)

Gillis 'Pastoral Poetry in Lucretius' *Latomus* 26 (1967) 339–62.

Goar, R.J., 'On the End of Lucretius' Fourth Book' *Classical Bulletin* 47 (1971) 75–7.

Gosling, J.C.B. and Taylor, C.C.W., *The Greeks on Pleasure* (Oxford 1982).

Graves, R., *The Greek Myths* (2nd ed. Harmondsworth 1960)

Griffin, A., *Sikyon* (Oxford 1982).

Griffin, J., 'Augustan Poetry and the Life of Luxury' *Journal of Roman Studies* 66 (1976) 87–105.

    'On the Relationship of Literature to Life' *Hesperiam* 4 (1981) 7–22.

Housman, A.E., 'Lucretiana' in *The Classical Papers of A.E. Housman*, ed. J. Diggle and F.R.D. Goodyear (Cambridg 1972) vol. 2. (1897–1914) pp 432–5.

Jenkyns, R., *Three Classical Poets* (London 1982).

Johns, C., *Sex or Symbol* (London 1982).

Kenney, E.J., 'Doctus Lucretius' *Mnemosyne* 23 (1970) 366–92.

— *Lucretius* (*Greece and Rome New Surveys in the Classics* 11 (1977)).

— 'The Key and the Cabinet: Ends and Means in Classical Studies' *Proceedings of the Classical Association* 80 (1983) 7–18.

Kerferd, G.B., *The Sophistic Movement* (Cambridge 1981).

Kinsey, T.E., 'The Melancholy of Lucretius' *Arion* 3 (1964) 115–30.

Kleve, K., 'Lucrèce, l'epicurisme et l'amour' *Association G. Bud⟨ Actes de Congres* VIII (Paris 1969) 376–83.

Laks, A. and Millot, C., 'Réexamen de quelque fragments de Diogène d'Oenoanda sur l'âme, la connaissance et la fortu⟨ *Études sur l'epicurisme Antique* (*Cahiers de Philologie* I (1976).

Lyne, R.O.A.M., *The Latin Love Poets* (Oxford 1980).

Macleod, C.W., Homer, *Iliad* 24 (Cambridge 1982).

Mewaldt 'Eine Dublette in Buch IV des Lukrez' *Hermes* 43 (1908) 286–95.

Minadeo, R., *The Lyre of Science* (Michigan 1969).

Momigliano, A., Review of Farrington: *Science and Politics in th⟨ Ancient World; Journal of Roman Studies* 31 (1941) 149–57

Muller, G., 'Die Finalia der sechs Bücher des Lukrez' in *Lucrèce (Fondation Hardt, Entretiens* 24 (1977) 197–231.

Nisbet, R.G., (ed.) *Cicero, In Pisonem* (Oxford 1961).

Nisbet, R.G. and Hubbard, M., *A Commentary on Horace Odes 1* (Oxford 1970).

Otto, A., *Die Sprichwörter und sprichwörtlichen Redensarten der Römer* (Leipzig 1890).

Paoli, U.E., *Rome; its People Life and Customs* (Aberdeen 1963)⟨

Paratore, E., 'La Problematica sull'epicureismo a Roma' in *Aufstieg und Niedergang der römischen Welt* (ed. Temporini) vol I.4 (1973) 116–204.

Paratore, H., *Lucreti De Rerum Natura locos praecipue notabiles collegit et illustravit,* (Rome 1960).

Perelli, L., *Lucrezio Poeta dell'Angoscia* (Firenze 1969).

Regenbogen, O., *Lukrez: seine Gestalt in seinem Gedicht* (Leipz 1932).

Reynolds, L.D. and Wilson, N.G., *Scribes and Scholars* (2nd edition Oxford 1974)

Richter, W., *Textstudien zu Lukrez* (Munich 1974).
Rist, J.M., *Epicurus, an Introduction* (Cambridge 1972).
Rosivach, V.J., 'Lucretius 4.1123-40' *American Journal of Philology*
    101 (1980) 401-3.
Sarsby, J., *Romantic Love and Society* (Harmondsworth 1983).
Schoenheim, U., 'The Place of *tactus* in Lucretius' *Philologus* 110
    (1966) 71-87.
Schrijvers, P.H., *Horror ac Divina Voluptas. Études sur la
    poétique et la poésie de Lucrèce* (Amsterdam 1970).
–   'La pensée de Lucrèce sur l'origine de la vie' *Mnemosyne*
    27 (1974) 245-61.
–   'La pensée d'Epicure et de Lucrèce sur le sommeil' *Études
    sur l'epicurisme antique* (*Cahiers de Philologie*) I (1976)
    231-59.
–   'Die Traumtheorie des Lukrez' *Mnemosyne* 33 (1980) 128-51.
Seaford, R., (ed) Euripides *Cyclops* (Oxford 1984).
Sedley, D., 'Epicurus and his professional Rivals' in *Études sur
    l'epicurisme antique* (*Cahiers de Philologie* I) (1976) 121-59.
    'On Signs' in *Science and Speculation* ed. Barnes, Burnyeat
    Brunschwig and Schofield (Cambridge 1982) 239-72.
Segal, E., *Roman Laughter* (Harvard 1968).
Snyder, J.M., *Puns and Poetry in Lucretius' de Rerum Natura*
    (Amsterdam 1980).
Sykes Davies, H., 'Notes on Lucretius' *Criterion* 11 (1931-2) 25-42.
Taladoire, B.A., '*Lucrèce devant l'amour*' *Annales de la Faculté
    des Lettres et Sciences Humaines de Nice* 21 (1974) 231-5.
Taylor, C.C.W., 'All perceptions are true' in (ed) Schofield,
    Burnyeat and Barnes, *Doubt and Dogmatism* (Oxford 1980)
    105-124.
Townend, G.B., 'Some problems of punctuation in the Latin
    Hexameter' *Classical Quarterly* 19 (1969) 330-44.
Traina, A., '*Dira libido* (sul linguaggio lucreziano dell Eros)'
    Studi di poesia latina in onore di A. Traglia (ed. di
    Storia) (Rome, 1979) 259-76.
Wallach, B.P., *Lucretius and the Diatribe against the Fear of Death:
    DRN 3.830-1094* (Leiden 1976).
Waszink, J.H., 'Lucretius and Poetry' *Mededelingen der
    koninklijke Nederlandse Akademie van Wetenschapen
    Afd. Letterkunde N.S.* 17 (1954) 243-57.
West, D.A., '*haurire, haustus* (Lucr.5.1069)' *Classical
    Quarterly* N.S. 15 (1965) 271-80.
–   *The Imagery and Poetry of Lucretius* (Edinburgh 1969).
–   'Lucretius' methods of argument (3.417-614)' *Classical
    Quarterly* 25 (1975) 94-116.

West, M.L., (ed) Hesiod *Theogony* (Oxford 1966).
Wilkinson, P.P., *The Georgics of Virgil* (Cambridge 1969).
Williams, G., *Tradition and Originality in Roman Poetry* (Oxford 1968).
Wiseman, T.P., 'The Two Worlds of Titus Lucretius' in *Cinna the Poet and other Roman Essays* (Leicester 1974) 11-43.

INTRODUCTION

Lucretius: Poet and Philosopher

Of Lucretius' life we know virtually nothing beyond that he was born in the 90's and died in the 50's B.C. Scholars, from St Jerome to T.P. Wiseman,[1] have attempted to construct a biography out of the poem itself in default of external evidence, prompted no doubt partly by the fascination of the silence of contemporary sources beyond a single sentence of Cicero (*ad Q.F.*1.10.3). In one sense the biographers are right; for Lucretius the writing of this poem *was* his life, if his dreams are anything to go by (4.969-70), and superficial details of his appearance and his parentage would be very small beer compared with the poetic testament he has left us, a poem which, more than any other, represents one man's view of existence with a life and colour no biography could match.

And yet it is still amazing that a poem of this size (at least[2] 7,415 lines) and artistry should have excited no remark among the poet's learned contemporaries, many of whom were Epicureans,[3] many more of whom were *literati*,[4] and some, such as Philodemus, both.[5] The romantic image of the lone voice crying in the wilderness or the recluse deranged by a love-potion, 'the long quiet of his breast' blasted 'with animal heat and dire insanity'[6] has been accepted right up to this century[7] in a variety of guises; some seeing him as an intellectual giant way ahead of his time, others putting him on the psychiatrist's couch and pronouncing him mentally unstable.[8]

These romantic theories are profoundly mistaken. Lucretius was not the only man to compose didactic verse in Rome – one has only to look at Cicero's translation of Aratus' *Phaenomena* and the fragments of Egnatius' *De Rerum Natura* to see the re-emergence of the didactic *epos* as a genre, taken up by no less a poet than Vergil in his *Georgics*. Writing didactic poetry was not the mark of a crank.[9] Nor was Epicureanism a freakish creed to follow; the anti-political stance espoused by Epicurus suited well the disillusion of the generation of Sulla and Marius, the pastoral idealism of Epicurus appealing to a generation which had more than once seen the streets flow with blood (cf 3.59f). Intellectually also, Epicureanism was highly respectable, influencing all the major

1

writers of the time, and leaving unmistakable traces in the work of Vergil and Horace.[10] Finally in literary terms the *De Rerum Natura* shows an awareness of both Greek and Latin literature both past and contemporary which gives the kiss of death to the notion of his exclusive obsession with 'those three hundred scrolls/ left by the teacher, whom he held divine'.[11] Of course he knew the works of Epicurus. He also seems to have known Homer, Greek Tragedy, Thucydides, Plato, the medical writers, Aristotle, the presocratic philosophers, Ennius, Roman and Greek Comedy, Greek Lyric and epigram, especially that of the Palatine Anthology, and possibly other writers whose works have not survived. The breadth and intensity of his intellectual curiosity are quite staggering. If all Roman literature is 'learned' (*doctus*),[12] Lucretius is so *par excellence*.

Learning, however, is not enough – as some of the Alexandrian writers demonstrated to their cost – and we should expect more than a mere stamp-collection of learned allusions from a poet aspiring to convey the truth about the world. The cultivation of technical virtuosity practised by the so-called metaphrasts (one thinks especially of Nicander), who turned scientific subject-matter into verse merely as a poetic *tour de force* without any real desire to inform or move the reader, differs *toto caelo* from Lucretius' passionate, personal involvement both with his subject-matter and with the reader's response. The technical virtuosity of the metaphrast is combined with all the devices of the rhetorician[13] for the ulterior, highly un-Alexandrian, purpose of changing the way we live. Philosophy for Lucretius was no ivory-tower, hermetic pursuit of useless ideas – his philosophy claimed to liberate man from illusions, and thus from fear bred of those illusions (the fear of death in particular), and thus also from the cruelty attendant upon superstitious terror (cf the sacrifice of Iphigeneia (1.80-101)) and the deluded pursuit of pleasure and power (3.59-86). The apparently misanthropic jeremiads against society (popular attitude to death (3.870ff); the romantic lover (4.1058-1191); superstitious fear of thunderbolts (6.379ff)) are born of sadness, not cynicism, and are essentially descriptive of how men in fact behave rather than prescriptive of how they ought; his strictures on the pursuit of pleasure are based on a clear, scientific assessment of the amount of 'real pleasure' (*vera voluptas* 5.1433) to be had, his attitude closer to Nietzsche's aphorism 'The mother of sensual excess is not joy, but rather the lack of joy' (*Menschliches*,

2

Allzumenschliches 2.77) than to that of a prurient kill-joy. Above all, the ethical imperatives of moderation and serenity are derived from close observation of the misery caused by frenzied excess, and the ideal of life is no less than *dignam dis degere vitam* – to live a life worthy of the gods (3.322).

Much of the above may occasion surprise in those accustomed to think of Epicurus as the preacher of atheistic hedonism, and it is important to know the elements of Epicurus' philosophy before embarking on the study of Lucretius. Epicurus lived from 341 to 270 B.C. and adopted the Atomist philosophy which had been developed by Democritus and Leucippus in the fifth century B.C. The essentials of the Atomist theory are very simple; everything that exists is material, and matter consists of tiny indivisible particles known as atoms (*a-tomoi* in Greek means indivisible). These atoms vary considerably in size, weight and shape, and it is the random combination of disparate atoms which gives rise to the array of phenomena we see, an important factor in the constitution of which is 'void' (*inane*, empty space) which combines with atoms in varying proportions to produce degrees of weight relative to size. Since void is by definition infinite, the universe itself (composed of atoms and nothingness) is also infinite, and our planet is but one of countless heavenly bodies which exist. The thorough-going materialism of atomist thought does not deny the existence of gods – on the contrary, Epicurus believed that they live a life of perfect tranquillity and detachment in the spaces between the worlds (*intermundia, metakosmia*), a paradigm of happiness which we can emulate. The essentially 'irreligious' nature of Epicureanism consists solely of his contention that the gods do not – indeed cannot – influence the affairs of men. Traditional superstitious beliefs that e.g. infertility is caused by the gods (4.1233ff) were anathema to Epicurus, who objected that the gods would hardly enjoy untroubled serenity if they were concerned with the petty problems of mankind; and since our concept of god presupposes the notion of perfection in happiness, the gods must *be* serene to be gods at all – an argument with all the flaws of the Ontological argument, but sincerely held none the less. Intercessionary prayer, sacrifice, curses and amulets are all a complete waste of time, urges Epicurus, both for the scientific reason that they cannot work and for the psychological reason that they only inculcate unhealthy desires and fears.

Epicurus' ethical system rested, as we have seen, on his

3

physics; if we are made up of atoms just like everything else, then our surest way to happiness is to recognise our true state and live within our physical means. This gives rise to what looks like Naturalism – the belief that ethical statements are ultimately translatable into scientific statements (usually of psychology) – with the implication that we can, like good machines, no more mend our ways than my car can fix its own engine; and this would clearly inhibit the scope of the preacher. There thus arises the very grey area of Free Will, explained by reference to the famous 'swerve' (*clinamen*) of the atoms (2.251-93) which introduces the vital element of unpredictability which is his answer to the determinism of his predecessor Democritus. We *are* moral beings with the ability to choose what we do, despite the automatic nature of many of our physical responses – 'both the brave man's and the coward's heart beat faster when the enemy's tanks begin to move forward, but only the coward deserts his post on the gun.'[14] Our natural inclination is towards pleasure and away from pain, which is not the same as saying that pleasure is the only thing worth seeking, for its own sake and in unbridled licentiousness. On the contrary, happiness depends upon an accurate perception of the world in which we recognise our limitations – the mortality of the soul, for instance – and also recognise that the essence of pleasure is not positive but negative, not the indulgence of sensual delectation but merely the cessation of pain. The choices we make will only lead to real happiness if they are informed with this degree of self-knowledge, culminating in the Epicurean paradox that 'real pleasure' will be found in the restriction of apparent pleasure to the *parvum quod satis est* (the little that is enough). If pleasure consists in the liberation from pain, then the ultimate pleasure will be in the total freedom from pain which is divine *ataraxia* or serenity.

This gives us an idea of the enormous ambition of the *De Rerum Natura*, a poem whose subject is everything and whose object is the liberation of man from pain. In the course of the six books which make up the poem Lucretius analyses: the nature of atoms and the void (Book 1) the properties and combinations of atoms in the diverse phenomena of the world (Book 2), the nature of the soul and its mortality (Book 3), the nature of our perception of the physical world, dreams, illusions and sex (Book 4) the history of the world and the development of mankind (Book 5) and a range of celestial and terrestrial phenomena, finishing with a description of the great plague of Athens (Book. 6). It is possible that Lucretius intended to add yet more to all this.[15] In writing the poem, Lucretius was conscious of a tradition that went back to Hesiod and was carried on by many of the great presocratic philosophers (cf his eulogy of Empedocles at 1.731-3),[16] a tradition which he took up despite the apparent hostility of Epicurus himself to poetry (though it is unlikely that Epicurus would have objected violently to a poem preaching his philosophy).[17] Lucretius' commitment to the poetic form is total.

Yet critics have often pointed to what they see as unevenness in his poetic style, brilliant 'purple passages' gleaming in the arid wastes of prosaic exegesis, fine moments (as Rossini said of Wagner) but tedious quarters of an hour. The dichotomy of Lucretius the poet and Lucretius the philosopher is often asserted in such crude terms, as if there were a universal poetic canon by which we measure degrees of 'poetry' – I find many of Auden's later poems considerably more prosaic than Lucretius, for instance, judged in this way; more importantly, the investigation of Lucretius' poetic style will get nowhere while we continue to think in terms of 'poetic digressions', forgetting the poet's unambiguous claim to 'coat *everything* with the elegance of the Muses' (4.9). That he did so has been demonstrated often enough now,[18] but let us take a passage from this book – more or less at random – to see the poet in action.

Lines 858-76 constitute a brief explanation of the mechanics of hunger and thirst. Lucretius explains that hunger is a natural reaction consequent upon the loss of atoms from the body, thirst is to maintain a constant temperature inside the body by cooling us down. Nothing very 'poetic' in any of that, it seems. Yet Lucretius develops both ideas into living metaphors, bringing them to life with astonishing immediacy. The loss of atoms from the body is explained in terms of a building which is undermined (*subruitur*); it needs shoring up with props (*suffulciat*) and the cracks need filling (*patentem obturet*). The bodily need for water is described in the language of putting out a fire (*incendia..restinguit ut ignem, urere*), the agony of thirst exaggerated with the violent image of a fire in the stomach. Nor is it only metaphor which brings the words off the page into life; there are the 'sound effects' of the panting animals in *exhalantur..languida anhelant* with its gasping assonance (repetition of the vowel a) and its repetition *-halant..-helant*, the hissing of the extinguished fire in *dissupat*; there are the 'verbalisations' of life, as in the expressive tmesis (splitting up) of *quaecumque* to suggest the wide spread of the thirsty parts of the body, and the effective juxtapositions of words – in 861, for instance, the pressure is deep down, so *ex alto pressa* is put together, and in 874 *aridus* is grammatically going with *calor* (dry heat), but is placed next to *artus* to suggest the dryness of the limbs which excessive thirst causes; there are the metrical sound-effects, such as the ramshackle, tumbling unevenness of 866 *quam consequitur rem* ending the line with a monosyllable; there are the effects of phrase-length and sentence construction, such as the long build-up of heat particles in 871-2 (*glomerataque..nostro*) with its semantic combustion of heat (*vaporis*) into fires (*incendia*) suddenly extinguished with the onomatopeiac verb *dissupat*, or the wide separation of *patentem/amorem* (gaping desire, sc. for food) with *per membra ac venas*, conveying both the extent of the gap verbally and the location of the need (throughout the limbs and veins) semantically; there are then the plays on words, such as his use of the periphrasis *corporis...natura* (858-9) picked up by *corpora* (860) – the 'body' needs food because 'bodies' keep leaving it – or the jingle of *amorem..umor* (869-70); there is extensive use in the passage of alliteration and assonance – an effect more appreciable when read aloud, as Roman literature was – such as *his igitur rebus rarescit*, or *restinguit ut ignem*; there is the device known as the tricolon crescendo (a group of three phrases building up in length and emphasis to a climax on the third) in 867-9: 1) *ut suffulciat artus* 2) *et recreet vires interdatus* 3) *atque patentem/per membra ac venas ut amorem obturet edendi*; there is the chiastic arrangement of *sitis* (A) *abluitur* (B) ..*expletur* (B)..*cupido* (A) which sets the two verbs in close proximity, producing a clash of imagery (flushing away vs filling up) but a similarity of form, just as hunger and thirst have different causes but are both alike involuntary mechanical reactions – as is brought out by the fact that both verbs are passive, not active (cf *capitur* 867). And so on. One could go on discovering new things, even in so short a passage, for a long time, without ever feeling that the topic had been exhausted. If we fail to see the poetry in Lucretius, as generations of readers appear to have done, that is not the poet's fault:

    quo magis in nobis, ut opinor, culpa resedit. (5.1425)

The fourth book of the _De Rerum Natura_ has often been written off as a farrago of incongruous topics, a book full of loose ends. In fact, of course, the internal coherence of the book is remarkably convincing, depending as it does on two basic ideas: the reliability of our senses and refutation of scepticism on the one hand, and the explanation of voluntary vs involuntary actions on the other. Throughout the book the reader is presented with the limitations of human experience and also the freedom to transcend them: thus we have a long section (26-822) explaining the physical nature of sensation, such that all perception, and even thought, is circumscribed by the images available and by our tendency to misjudge things (as in the list of optical illusions 379-468); and yet the centrepiece of this section is a witty rebuttal of the sceptic's assertion that we know nothing. Our senses _are_ limited, Lucretius argues - but we are still free to see what is there, if we _know_ the limitations we are working with. The section from 823-1057 (despairingly entitled by Bailey 'Some functions of the body considered in connexion with psychology') is again a cluster of proofs of our limitations centred around a declaration of our freedom to choose whether to move ourselves or not. This is the relevance of the anti-teleological section (823-57), (described by Bailey as a digression); to assert that our freedom to act is limited by the means available, and that our bodies are not _designed_ to cope with the world but that they have developed slowly to a point where they can; our physical need to eat and drink, our involuntary tendency to sleep, our inability to prevent ourselves from dreaming, once asleep, and the involuntary emission of semen during sleep are all likewise examples of the 'non-voluntary' side of our nature,[19] but they do not discredit our deeper freedom to _move_ - a freedom which has moral, as well as physical, implications.[20] As with sense-perception, our freedom is restricted by our faculties (823-57) and our bodily needs (858-76, 907-1057), but our slender thread of free will remains, relying on what is 'given' (i.e. the available images which inform thought) but transcending the mechanical with a spark of the spontaneous.

These two strands are brought together into the disquisition on love and sex which closes the book. On the one hand, we are bound to produce semen which will need release, and as animals we need to reproduce ourselves - so much is beyond our control; but as individuals we have a choice of

7

pursuing sanity or madness. What does this 'madness' consist in? Lucretius, as indeed virtually all the ancients (see note on 1069), regarded madness as essentially hallucination, the failure to see what is really there. Thus the whole thrust of the argument at the close of the book is a specific application of the principle expounded so thoroughly early in the book – that our senses are reliable, but our minds must be trained to interpret the evidence correctly. Romantic love is an optical illusion, no less than seeing square towers as round, in that the romantic lover sees his ugly girlfriend as the paragon of beauty. His refusal to perceive the truth leads him to fight against both the sexual demands of human nature, in that his worship of the 'mistress' entails retaining his sperm rather than releasing it (1066) and his unrequited love could never become the kind of reproductive union the poet endorses at the end of the book – if he ever got close enough to her, the lover would flee in disgust (1180ff). The scenario is of course fixed by Lucretius, such that the lover can't win – he cannot achieve union with his beloved, because she won't allow him, but even if he did it would be hopeless in view of his impossible expectations of what this 'ideal woman' is really like – but then it is the lover's fault for indulging his illusions in the first place.

So at the end of the book we come to an ethical conclusion based on physical premises; sanity is a matter of seeing straight, and happiness consists in the assuaging of our physical desires in the most honest and direct way. Therefore we must not idealise individual women as being 'more than mortal' (1184), both because it would fly in the face of reason to do so and also because it would limit our scope for sexual release to such an extent that pain would be virtually inevitable. The book closes with a strong suggestion that sexual needs can be satisfied in the context of a friendship born of habit – and friendship was the highest good, according to Epicurus –, a reminder that pleasure is maximised when our desires are fewest, and so the 'homely little woman' would be ideal for the wise man who practises moderation in all things; and finally an analogy from the natural world tells us yet again that in an entirely atomic universe, happiness and sanity alike will depend on our recognition of the limitations imposed by nature upon us, as upon everything else.

Finally, the prologue's relevance to all this is also secure. In the famous simile of the doctor attempting to administer medicine to sick children we have a paradigm of

8

human nature blindly and immaturely following its instincts rather than the light of reason. The child has the choice of taking the medicine or not, but the medicine, once taken, will work (or not) independent of the wishes of the patient; thus already we see adumbrated the themes of freedom vs limitation which will dominate the book. Now the child will only be cured by *deceit* of his senses - in contrast to the poet's insistence later on that freedom requires the veracity of the senses - and yet the coherence remains convincing precisely because we have been *told* of the 'deceit', thus inviting the reader into the whole truth about the world. And part of that truth, Lucretius will tell us in great and vivid detail, is that our limitations will prevent us ever seeing all of it.

The Transmission of the Text

There are two main manuscripts of the *De Rerum Natura*, Oblongus (O) and Quadratus (Q), both housed in the University Library in Leiden, Holland. They were written in France in the ninth century A.D., and derive from a common original written in capitals in the fourth or the fifth century. The third strand of the manuscript tradition is the Italian family of manuscripts, all deriving from a lost manuscript (P) which was discovered by the Italian Humanist Poggio Bracciolini, copied by him, and lost again. Poggio's copy is also now lost, but the copy of Poggio's copy (p) made by another Humanist, Niccolo de' Niccoli, survives in the Laurentian Library in Florence. (p) and L (Niccolo's copy) are the source of all the Italian copies of Lucretius made in the fifteenth century, as they are of all other manuscripts which survive, excepting the fragmentary ninth-century G-V and U, neither of which contains Book 4. The chief problem in the textual tradition of Lucretius is in determining the relationship of the OQG-VU set of manuscripts to the Italian tradition of (P); it has recently been argued persuasively by Konrad Müller that (P) derives from O,[21] and that thus all the Italian manuscripts are dependent on the OQG-VU tradition.

In constituting the text of this edition I have endeavoured to produce continuous sense by plugging gaps whenever possible (though *lacunae* such as 126*7 proved quite impossible to plug) and emending *cruces* with a confidence that may seem rash, on the grounds that readability is of more consequence than authenticity when authenticity would mean printing nonsense. All emendations which differ markedly from the readings of other available texts are marked in the *apparatus criticus*.

NOTES TO INTRODUCTION

1. See Wiseman.
2. There are gaps in the text (*lacunae*) where it is almost certain that a whole page of the archetype has been lost (e.g. 4.126*7).
3. See Momigliano 151-7.
4. Such as Catullus and his circle of 'neoterics' with whom L had more affinity than has been recognised; see Ferrero.
5. On Philodemus and his associates see Nisbet (1961) Appendix 3, 183-6.
6. Tennyson, *Lucretius*.
7. Well-discussed - and refuted - by T.E. Kinsey.
8. For the former, see Regenbogen 15; for the latter, see Perelli.
9. See Brown (1982) 77-8.
10. On Vergil, see (e.g.) Wilkinson 63-5; on Horace, Fraenkel 253ff.
11. Tennyson *Lucretius*.
12. See Kenney (1983).
13. See Classen.
14. D.J. Furley (1967) 222.
15. On the vexed question of whether the *DRN* is complete or not, see Kenney (1977) 22.
16. For a brief survey of the genre of the Didactic *epos* see Cox (1969) 124-61.
17. For the hostility of Epicurus to poetry - if it existed - see Waszink.
18. e.g. Sykes Davies, and Amory.
19. cf. Aristotle *De Motu Animalium* 703b 5ff; Furley (1967) 210-26.
20. See ref. at n 14 above.
21. K. Muller *Mus.Helv.* 30 (1973) 166-78.

DE RERUM NATURA

Book IV

avia Pieridum peragro loca nullius ante
trita solo. iuvat integros accedere fontis
atque haurire, iuvatque novos decerpere flores
insignemque meo capiti petere inde coronam
unde prius nulli velarint tempora Musae: 5
primum quod magnis doceo de rebus et artis
religionum animum nodis exsolvere pergo,
deinde quod obscura de re tam lucida pango
carmina, musaeo contingens cuncta lepore.
id quoque enim non ab nulla ratione videtur;   10
nam veluti pueris absinthia taetra medentes
cum dare conantur, prius oras pocula circum
contingunt mellis dulci flavoque liquore,
ut puerorum aetas inprovida ludificetur
labrorum tenus, interea perpotet amarum   15
absinthi laticem deceptaque non capiatur,
sed potius tali tactu recreata valescat,
sic ego nunc, quoniam haec ratio plerumque videtur
tristior esse quibus non est tractata, retroque
volgus abhorret ab hac, volui tibi suaviloquenti   20
carmine Pierio rationem exponere nostram
et quasi musaeo dulci contingere melle,
si tibi forte animum tali ratione tenere
versibus in nostris possem, dum percipis omnem
naturam rerum ac persentis utilitatem.   25

atque animi quoniam docui natura quid esset
et quibus e rebus cum corpore compta vigeret
quove modo distracta rediret in ordia prima,
nunc agere incipiam tibi, quod vehementer ad has res
attinet, esse ea quae rerum simulacra vocamus;   30
quae, quasi membranae summo de corpore rerum
dereptae, volitant ultroque citroque per auras,
atque eadem nobis vigilantibus obvia mentes
terrificant atque in somnis, cum saepe figuras
contuimur miras simulacraque luce carentum,   35

---

17 tactu *Lambinus* (1570): atacto *OQ*: a tactu *L*: pacto *Heinsius*

12

I range over the trackless terrain of the Muses, an area no man's foot has trodden before. I love to make for untouched springs and draw from them, I love to pluck new flowers and seek from them a crown of glory for my head, from fields whence until now no other man's temples have been wreathed by the Muses. First because I teach 5 about important matters – my ambition is to untie the mind from the tight knots of religious beliefs. Secondly because, though my subject is dark, the songs I compose are so light, as I coat everything with the elegance of the Muses. Nor does this seem devoid of purpose: for 10 just as when doctors are trying to administer foul-tasting wormwood to children, they first smear the rims of the cups all round with the sweet yellow syrup of honey, so that the children in their youthful naivety should have this prank played upon them, as far as their lips; so that 15 before they know it they will drink up all the sour wormwood juice and thus be tricked but not sickened, but rather recover and grow strong by this contact. This is my intention now, since this philosophy is regarded for the most part as too sour by those who have not handled it, and the masses shrink back from it in horror; so I 20 wanted to lay out our philosophy for you in the pleasant-voiced song of the Muses, to coat it, as it were, with the Muses' sweet honey, to see if I could thus hold your attention fixed on our verses, while you are grasping the universal nature of things and while you are feeling the full value of doing so. 25

Since I have already taught you about the nature of mind, the elements from which it is composed in its healthy union with the body, and the manner in which it is torn apart and returns to its constituent parts, now I shall begin to broach a subject of strong relevance to this, namely the existence of what we call 'images' of 30 objects. These images are like skins stripped from the outermost body-surface of things, which fly back and forth through the breezes. It is these same images which terrify our minds when they strike us, both when we are awake and in sleep, when we often gaze on amazing forms and images of the light-lacking dead, images which have 35

13

quae nos horrifice languentis saepe sopore
excierunt; ne forte animas Acherunte reamur
effugere aut umbras inter vivos volitare
neve aliquid nostri post mortem posse relinqui,
cum corpus simul atque animi natura perempta   40
in sua discessum dederint primordia quaeque.
dico igitur rerum effigias tenuisque figuras
mittier ab rebus summo de cortice rerum;
id licet hinc quamvis hebeti cognoscere corde.
[sed quoniam docui cunctarum exordia rerum   45
qualia sint et quam variis distantia formis
sponte sua volitent aeterno percita motu
quoque modo possit res ex his quaeque creari,
nunc agere incipiam tibi, quod vehementer ad has res
attinet, esse ea quae rerum simulacra vocamus,   50
quae quasi membranae vel cortex nominitandast,
quod speciem ac formam similem gerit eius imago
cuiuscumque cluet de corpore fusa vagari.]

principio quoniam mittunt in rebus apertis
corpora res multae, partim diffusa solute,   55
robora ceu fumum mittunt ignesque vaporem,
et partim contexta magis condensaque, ut olim
cum teretis ponunt tunicas aestate cicadae,
et vituli cum membranas de corpore summo
nascentes mittunt, et item cum lubrica serpens   60
exuit in spinis vestem; nam saepe videmus
illorum spoliis vepres volitantibus auctas.
quae quoniam fiunt, tenuis quoque debet imago
ab rebus mitti summo de corpore rerum.
nam cur illa cadant magis ab rebusque recedant   65
quam quae tenvia sunt, hiscendist nulla potestas,
praesertim cum sint in summis corpora rebus
multa minuta, iaci quae possint ordine eodem
quo fuerint et formai servare figuram,
et multo citius, quanto minus indupediri   70

_____

42 effigias *Lambinus* : effugias *OQ*
43 cortice *OQ* : corpore *Lambinus* : rerum *Lachmann* : eorum
OQ
53 cluet *ed. Brix.* : cui et *O* : civet *Q*
69 formai *Vossius* : forma *OQ* : cum forma *Q¹* : conformem
Lambinus

14

often wakened us up with horror as we lay slothful in sleep. There is a danger of us perhaps thinking that spirits escape from the Underworld, or ghosts flit among the living; or we might think some part of us can be left surviving after death, when both the body and the mind   40
have been disintegrated, have taken their leave and returned each to their own constituent atoms. My claim, then, is that copies and thin shapes of objects are discharged from their outermost surface skin – a claim that anyone, however dull his brain, may understand from what follows. (But since I have explained the nature   45
of the primary parts of all things, how they differ, how varied their forms, how they fly without any external compulsion yet driven by eternal motion, how each and every material thing can be fashioned out of these primary atoms, now I shall begin to broach a subject of strong relevance to this, namely the existence of what we call 'images' of things, which should be called, as it   50
were, their 'skins' or 'bark', since the image wears an appearance and form similar to the object – whatever it is – which discharged it on its travels.)
First of all,   there are many   perceptible cases of things giving off particles, some of them dissolved and scattered   55
abroad, such as wood giving off smoke and fires giving off heat, others more closely woven and condensed, as at those times when cicadas drop their smooth shirts in summer, or when new-born calves shed the filmy skins from their body surface, or again when the slippery   60
snake divests himself of his clothing on thorns – for we often see brambles enriched by these fluttering scalps. Since these things happen, a fine image must also be sloughed off the outer body-surface of things; for why   65
should those (coarse) things be more likely to fall off, to come away from things, than those things which are insubstantial? This is especially incontrovertible since there are many tiny bodies on the surfaces of things, bodies which could be thrown off in the same position they were in before, could thus preserve the shape of their form, and do so much more swiftly inasmuch as they are few in number and marshalled on the front line, and thus are less likely to be obstructed.   70

pauca queunt et quae sunt prima fronte locata.
nam certe iacere ac largiri multa videmus,
non solum ex alto penitusque, ut diximus ante,
verum de summis ipsum quoque saepe colorem.
et volgo faciunt id lutea russaque vela   75
et ferrugina, cum magnis intenta theatris
per malos volgata trabesque trementia flutant;
namque ibi consessum caveai subter et omnem
scaenai speciem personarumque decorem
inficiunt coguntque suo fluitare colore.   80
et quanto circum mage sunt inclusa theatri
moenia, tam magis haec intus perfusa lepore
omnia conrident correpta luce diei.
ergo lintea de summo cum corpore fucum
mittunt, effigias quoque debent mittere tenvis   85
res quaeque, ex summo quoniam iaculantur utraque.
sunt igitur iam formarum vestigia certa
quae volgo volitant subtili praedita filo,
nec singillatim possunt secreta videri.
praeterea omnis odor fumus vapor atque aliae res   90
consimiles ideo diffusae e rebus abundant,
ex alto quia dum veniunt intrinsecus ortae,
scinduntur per iter flexum, nec recta viarum
ostia sunt qua contendant exire coortae.
at contra tenuis summi membrana coloris   95
cum iacitur, nil est quod eam discerpere possit,
in promptu quoniam est in prima fronte locata.
postremo speculis in aqua splendoreque in omni
quaecumque apparent nobis simulacra, necessest,
quandoquidem simili specie sunt praedita rerum,   100
ex ea imaginibus missis consistere rerum.   101
sunt igitur tenues formarum consimilesque   104
effigiae, singillatim quas cernere nemo   105
cum possit, tamen adsiduo crebroque repulsu
reiectae reddunt speculorum ex aequore visum,

---

71 quae sunt *Lachmann*: sunt *OQ*
72 ac largiri *Lachmann*: aciergiri *OQ*: ac iaculari *l. 31*
79 personarumque decorem *K. Müller*: patrum matrumque
deorum *OQ*: pulcram variamque deorsum *W. Richter*
92 intrinsecus *Lambinus*: extrinsecus *OQ*
101 ea *add. Lotze*: 102–3 = 65–66.
104 formarum consimilesque *Lambinus*: formarum
dissimilesque *OQ*: formarum illis similesque *Lachmann*

16

For we see many things throwing out particles prodigally,
not only from deep down inside them, as we said before,
but also from the surfaces, as often colour itself. Yellow,   75
red and purple canvasses do this often, when they are
stretched out in great theatres, spread tight over masts
and beams: they tremble and flutter and dye the seated
throng in the hollow below them, the whole spectacle of
the stage and the magnificence of the masked actors,
forcing them to ripple in their own colours. Further, the   80
more the walls of the theatre are enclosed, the more the
light of day is reduced, and everything inside the walls
is bathed in beauty and laughs. So, since canvasses emit
dye from their body surface, it must follow that all things   85
emit fine images, as in each case particles are discharged
from the surface. Therefore definite traces of shapes
exist, delicately woven, which flitter abroad, but cannot
be seen individually as discrete entities.

Next, the reason why all smell, smoke, heat and the like   90
pour out of matter spreading widely is that they have
arisen deep within the object; in coming from inside they
are cut to pieces on their winding journey, as there are
no direct openings to roads on which they could leave
marching in step as a unit. On the other hand, when a   95
thin skin of surface colour is thrown off, there is nothing
to tear it, since it is ready positioned in the front line.

Finally, whatever images appear to us in mirrors, water
or any bright surface, all have an outward appearance   100
similar to the objects themselves; they must therefore be
formed from images discharged from the objects. There
thus exist insubstantial replicas of forms, accurate   105
copies, which, though nobody could perceive them
individually, yet when bounced back in constant, quick

nec ratione alia servari posse vidèntur,
tanto opere ut similes reddantur cuique figurae.

nunc age quam tenui natura constet imago   110
percipe. et in primis, quoniam primordia tantum
sunt infra nostros sensus tantoque minora
quam quae primum oculi coeptant non posse tueri,
nunc tamen id quoque uti confirmem, exordia rerum
cunctarum quam sint subtilia percipe paucis.   115
primum animalia sunt iam partim tantula, eorum ut
tertia pars nulla possit ratione videri.
horum intestinum quodvis quale esse putandumst?
quid cordis globus aut oculi? quid membra? quid artus?
quantula sunt? quid praeterea primordia quaeque   120
unde anima atque animi constet natura necessumst?
nonne vides quam sint subtilia quamque minuta?
praeterea quaecumque suo de corpore odorem
expirant acrem, panaces absinthia taetra
habrotonique graves et tristia centaurea,   125
quorum unum quidvis leviter si forte duobus

                          *

quin potius noscas rerum simulacra vagari
multa modis multis nulla vi cassaque sensu?

sed ne forte putes ea demum sola vagari,
quaecumque ab rebus rerum simulacra recedunt,   130
sunt etiam quae sponte sua gignuntur et ipsa
constituuntur in hoc caelo qui dicitur aer,
quae multis formata modis sublime feruntur;   (135)
ut nubes facile interdum concrescere in alto   (133)
cernimus et mundi speciem violare serenam,   135   (134)
aera mulcentes motu; nam saepe Gigantum
ora volare videntur et umbram ducere late,
interdum magni montes avolsaque saxa
montibus anteire et solem succedere praeter,
inde alios trahere atque inducere belua nimbos.   140
nec speciem mutare suam liquentia cessant
et cuiusque modi formarum vertere in oras.

_____

116 eorum ut *l. 31*: eorum *OQ*: quorum *Purmann*
126*127 *lacunam cruce notat Q¹*
133 (135) *transposuit Lambinus*

reflection they produce a visible image from the smooth surface of mirrors; nor does there seem any other way in which the images can be preserved so that such faithful representations of individual shapes can be reflected.

Come now, and grasp how tenuous is the structure of the image. Firstly, since the atoms are so far below our powers of sensation, so much smaller than the largest things that are too small for our eyes to see, and to prove this also, grasp now in a few words how finely textured are the elements of all things. First of all, there are some living things which are so tiny that, if divided into thirds, they could not be seen at all. What should we suppose one of their intestines is like? Or the ball of their heart or eyes? Their bodily parts? Their limbs? How tiny are they? What then of the individual atoms that must make up their spirit and mind? Don't you see how fine-textured, how minute they are? Besides, all the things which breathe out a pungent smell from their body – all-healing catholicon, bitter wormwood, oppressive southernwood, rank centaury – take any of these lightly between two (fingers, and the smell will cling to them, although the particles which cling to them are invisible.) ... but that you should realise that images of objects wander abroad in great numbers in many different ways, powerless and imperceptible.

But to prevent you thinking that the images which emanate from objects are the only images wandering abroad, remember that there are also those images which are produced spontaneously and form themselves in this part of the sky which we call the air, images which are shaped in a wide variety of ways and are borne aloft; just as we sometimes see clouds effortlessly merging together on high, staining the tranquil appearance of the firmament, caressing the air with their movement; for often Giants' faces seem to be flying, drawing their shadow over a great distance, and sometimes massive mountains and rocks torn from mountains seem to march ahead of, and then pass over, the sun; and then a monster seems to be dragging other clouds, black storm-clouds, behind him. They never stop dissolving and changing their appearance, turning into the outlines of every manner of shape.

nunc ea quam facili et celeri ratione genantur
perpetuoque fluant ab rebus lapsaque cedant
(expediam: tu te dictis praebere memento.)   (2.66)
semper enim summum quicquid de rebus abundat   145
quod iaculentur. et hoc alias cum pervenit in res
(non eadem patitur semper: nam limpida quae sunt)   146a
transit, ut in primis vitrum. sed ubi aspera saxa
aut in 'materiam ligni pervenit, ibi iam
scinditur, ut nullum simulacrum reddere possit.
at cum splendida quae constant opposta fuerunt   150
densaque, ut in primis speculum est, nil accidit horum;
nam neque, uti vitrum, possunt transire, neque autem
scindi; quam meminit levor praestare salutem.
quapropter fit ut hinc nobis simulacra redundent.
et quamvis subito quovis in tempore quamque   155
rem contra speculum ponas, apparet imago;
perpetuo fluere ut noscas e corpore summo
texturas rerum tenuis tenuisque figuras.
ergo multa brevi spatio simulacra genuntur,
ut merito celer his rebus dicatur origo.   160
et quasi multa brevi spatio summittere debet
lumina sol ut perpetuo sint omnia plena,
sic ab rebus item simili ratione necessest
temporis in puncto rerum simulacra ferantur
multa modis multis in cunctas undique partis,   165
quandoquidem speculum quocumque obvertimus, omnis
res ibi respondent simili forma atque colore.
praeterea modo cum fuerit liquidissima caeli
tempestas, perquam subito fit turbida foede,
undique uti tenebras omnis Acherunta rearis   170
liquisse et magnas caeli complesse cavernas:
usque adeo taetra nimborum nocte coorta
inpendent atrae formidinis ora superne;
quorum quantula pars sit imago dicere nemost
qui possit neque eam rationem reddere dictis.   175
nunc age, quam celeri motu simulacra ferantur
et quae mobilitas ollis tranantibus auras
reddita sit, longo spatio ut brevis hora teratur,

144*145 lacunam indicavit Lachmann
146 alias OQ: certas Brieger: laxas Merrill: 146a
scripsit W. Richter
147 vitrum Oppenrieder vestem OQ
166 omnis Voss: oris Q:om.O

Now I shall explain to you the facility and speed with
which these images are produced, flowing perpetually
from objects, slipping off them and taking their leave;
you remember to pay attention to my words.
For there is always something on the outermost surface   145
flowing away from things for them to fire off. When this
discharge reaches other material objects (it does not
always suffer the same fate: for things which are
transparent) it passes through, as it does especially in
the case of glass. But when it reaches rough rocks or
solid wood, it is chopped up there and then, preventing
the transmission of any image. But when it encounters   150
those things that are bright and solid, a mirror in
particular, then neither of these things happens: for the
images cannot pass through it, like glass, neither can
they be chopped up – for the smoothness guarantees their
safety without needing to be reminded.
That is why images flow back to us from these surfaces.
Nor does it matter how suddenly, at what time, or what   155
object you set up facing the mirror – the image appears.
This should make you realise that there is a constant
stream of flimsy textures, flimsy shapes flowing from the
surface of things. Therefore images are produced in great   160
numbers in a short space of time, their origin being
justifiably termed 'rapid'. The sun must emit many rays
of light in a short space of time, to ensure that all things
are permanently filled: similarly, the images of things
must be transported away in a moment of time, in great   165
numbers and many different ways in all directions
everywhere, since, whichever way we turn the mirror,
everything answers back there with similar shape and
colour. Besides, even when the weather in the sky has
just now been extremely clear, with amazing suddenness
it turns severely stormy, to make you think that all the   170
darkness had left the Underworld and filled the great
caverns of the sky: to such an extent has the hideous
night of storm-clouds gathered and faces of dark fear
hang down over us. Yet nobody could say, or explain in
words, how tiny a part of these things the image is.   175
Come now: how swift is the motion with which the images
travel, what velocity has been imparted to them as they
swim through the breezes, such that only a short hour is

in quem quaeque locum diverso numine tendunt,
suavidicis potius quam multis versibus edam;   180
parvus ut est cycni melior canor, ille gruum quam ⎫ 909-11
clamor in aetheriis dispersus nubibus austri.   ⎭
principio persaepe levis res atque minutis
corporibus factas celeris licet esse videre.
in quo iam genere est solis lux et vapor eius,   185
propterea quia sunt e primis facta minutis
quae quasi cuduntur perque aeris intervallum
non dubitant transire sequenti concita plaga;
suppeditatur enim confestim lumine lumen,
et quasi protelo stimulatur fulgere fulgur.   190
quapropter simulacra pari ratione necesse est
inmemorabile per spatium transcurrere posse
temporis in puncto, primum quod parvola causa
est procul a tergo quae provehat atque propellat,
quod superest, ubi tam volucri levitate ferantur;   195
deinde quod usque adeo textura praedita rara
mittuntur, facile ut quasvis penetrare queant res
et quasi permanare per aeris intervallum.
praeterea si quae penitus corpuscula rerum
ex altoque foras mittuntur, solis uti lux   200
ac vapor, haec puncto cernuntur lapsa diei
per totum caeli spatium diffundere sese
perque volare mare ac terras caelumque rigare,
quid quae sunt igitur iam prima fronte parata,
cum iaciuntur et emissum res nulla moratur?   205
quone vides citius debere et longius ire
multiplexque loci spatium transcurrere eodem
tempore quo solis pervolgant lumina caelum?
hoc etiam in primis specimen verum esse videtur
quam celeri motu rerum simulacra ferantur,   210
quod simul ac primum sub diu splendor aquai
ponitur, extemplo caelo stellante serena
sidera respondent in aqua radiantia mundi.
iamne vides igitur quam puncto tempore imago
aetheris ex oris in terrarum accidat oras?   215
quare etiam atque etiam mira fateare necessest

*

---

179 numine *OQ*: momine *Marullus*
216 mira *O*: ira *Q*: mitti *Lachmann: post 216 lacunam
indicavit Purmann*

22

wasted on a long journey, in whatever direction they each travel with their different inclinations; all this will I proclaim in verses that are more mellifluous than multitudinous; just as the brief song of the swan is preferable to that noise of cranes broadcast among the southern clouds in the sky.

Firstly, you may notice very often how things which are light and composed of tiny particles are swift. The light and the heat of the sun fall in this category because they are made of tiny elements which are, as it were, beaten and so do not hesitate to pass through the space of air intervening, driven on by the blow which follows them; for light is instantly supplied with light, flash is goaded on by flash, as in a team of yoked animals. So in like manner must images be able to run through a stupendous distance in an instant; first because there is a tiny little impulse far off behind them which carries and drives them on, then because they travel with such bird-swift lightness, and then because they are discharged with such a loosely-woven texture that they can easily pierce through any object and, as it were, ooze through the intervening air. Besides, if there are particles of matter which are sent out from deep down inside – such as the light and heat of the sun – which are yet seen to slip and pour themselves through the whole space of heaven in a single moment of the day, to fly through the sea and lands and flood the sky, what then of those which are already stationed on the front line when they are thrown off, with nothing to delay their discharge? Do you see how much faster and farther they must travel, how they must run through an extent of space many times vaster in the time it takes the light of the sun to spread throughout the sky? This also seems especially compelling evidence for the rapidity of movement of the images of things: as soon as the brightness of water is placed under the open sky when stars are visible in the heavens, at once the heavenly bodies of the firmament in their tranquillity answer back gleaming in the water. Now do you see, then, how in a single instant the image falls from the shores of the upper air to the shores of the earth?

corpora quae feriant oculos visumque lacessant.
perpetuoque fluunt certis ab rebus odores;
frigus ut a fluviis, calor ab sole, aestus ab undis
aequoris exesor moerorum litora circum;   220
nec variae cessant voces volitare per auras;
denique in os salsi venit umor saepe saporis,
cum mare versamur propter, dilutaque contra
cum tuimur misceri absinthia, tangit amaror.
usque adeo omnibus ab rebus res quaeque fluenter   225
fertur et in cunctas dimittitur undique partis,
nec mora nec requies interdatur ulla fluendi,
perpetuo quoniam sentimus, et omnia semper
cernere odorari licet et sentire sonare.
praeterea quoniam manibus tractata figura   230
in tenebris quaedam cognoscitur esse eadem quae
cernitur in luce et claro candore, necessest
consimili causa tactum visumque moveri.
nunc igitur si quadratum temptamus et id nos
commovet in tenebris, in luci quae poterit res   235
accidere ad speciem quadrata nisi eius imago?
esse in imaginibus quapropter causa videtur
cernundi neque posse sine his res ulla videri.
nunc ea quae dico rerum simulacra feruntur
undique et in cunctas iaciuntur didita partis;   240
verum nos oculis quia solis cernere quimus,
propterea fit uti, speciem quo vertimus, omnes
res ibi eam contra feriant forma atque colore.
et quantum quaeque ab nobis res absit, imago
efficit ut videamus et internoscere curat;   245
nam cum mittitur, extemplo protrudit agitque
aera qui inter se cumque est oculosque locatus,
isque ita per nostras acies perlabitur omnis
et quasi perterget pupillas atque ita transit.
propterea fit uti videamus quam procul absit   250 (251
res quaeque; et quanto plus aeris ante agitatur   (250
et nostros oculos perterget longior aura,
tam procul esse magis res quaeque remota videtur.
scilicet haec summe celeri ratione geruntur,
quale sit ut videamus et una quam procul absit.   255

All the more reason why one has to admit that (the images move) with amazing (speed) ....
... bodies which strike the eyes and provoke vision. Some things have smells permanently flowing from them, like cold from rivers, heat from the sun, spray from the waves of the sea which gnaws away at the walls around the shore. 220
Then all kinds of voices never stop flying through the breezes; again, fluid with a salty flavour often comes into the mouth when we are walking by the sea, and when we are watching wormwood being mixed with water at close quarters, the bitterness of it touches us. To this extent 225
each individual quality travels in a stream from all things and is spread in all directions everywhere, with no delay or respite granted to interrupt the flow since our perception is unbroken and we can at any time see anything, smell anything and feel it sound. Besides, a 230
shape that is felt with the hands in the dark is recognisably the same as that which is seen in the light in its brilliant brightness; it follows that touch and sight must be moved by a similar cause. Thus if we are handling something square, and it moves our sense of 235
touch in the darkness, when we are in the light what square thing will be able to strike our sense of sight except the image of that thing? Therefore the cause of sight is seen to reside in images, without which nothing is visible.
Now the images of things which I am talking about are carried everywhere, discharged and dispersed in all 240
directions; but because we can see only with our eyes it happens that all things beat upon our sense of sight with their shape and colour only at the place where we direct our gaze.
The image also makes us see, taking care that we mark the distinctions, how far each thing is distant from us. 245
For, when it is discharged, it at once shoves forward and drives on whatever air is placed between itself and our eyes, so that this air all slides through our eyes and, as it were, brushes through our pupils on its way. That is 250
how we come to see how far away each separate thing is; the more air is stirred up in front of it, and the longer the breeze which brushes through our eyes, the further away each object is seen to be removed. Of course these things happen with the utmost speed, so that we gauge the distance at the same moment that we see the object. 255

25

illud in his rebus minime mirabile habendumst,
cur, ea quae feriant oculos simulacra videri
singula cum nequeant, res ipsae perspiciantur.
ventus enim quoque paulatim cum verberat et cum
acre fluit frigus, non privam quamque solemus   260   (261
particulam venti sentire et frigoris eius,   (260)
sed magis unorsum, fierique perinde videmus
corpore tum plagas in nostro tamquam aliquae res
verberet atque sui det sensum corporis extra.
praeterea lapidem digito cum tundimus, ipsum   265
tangimus extremum saxi summumque colorem,
nec sentimus eum tactu, verum magis ipsam
duritiem penitus saxi sentimus in alto.
nunc age, cur ultra speculum videatur imago
percipe: nam certe penitus remmota videtur.   270
quod genus illa foris quae vere transpiciuntur,
ianua cum per se transpectum praebet apertum,
multa facitque foris ex aedibus ut videantur;
is quoque enim duplici geminoque fit aere visus:
primus enim citra postes tum cernitur aer,   275
inde fores ipsae dextra laevaque sequuntur,
post extraria lux oculos perterget et aer
alter et illa foris quae vere transpiciuntur.
sic ubi se primum speculi proiecit imago,
dum venit ad nostras acies, protrudit agitque   280
aera qui inter se cumquest oculosque locatus,
et facit ut prius hunc omnem sentire queamus
quam speculum: sed ubi speculum quoque sensimus ipsum,
continuo a nobis itidem quae fertur imago
pervenit, et nostros oculos reiecta revisit,   285
atque alium prae se propellens aera volvit,
et facit ut prius hunc quam se videamus, eoque
distare ab speculo tantum semota videtur.
quare etiam atque etiam minime mirarier est par
(hoc illis fieri, quae transpiciuntur, idemque)   289a
illis quae reddunt speculorum ex aequore visum,   290
aeribus binis quoniam res confit utraque.

---

270 remmota Q: remota O: semota Marullus
284 itidem C.L. Howard: in eum OQ: in idem Munro:
in id haec Lambinus (1570)
289*290 lacunam indicavit Goebel
289a scripsit Bailey

26

Now in this topic there should be no need to wonder why it is that things themselves are perceived but the images which strike the eyes are individually invisible. For when the wind is lashing us bit by bit, and when biting cold   260
flows at us we do not usually feel each separate particle of that wind and that cold, but rather the whole thing at once, and we see that the blows occur upon our body exactly as if some single thing outside the body were beating us and making its presence felt. Besides, when   265
we stub our toe upon a stone it is only the topmost part of the stone, the outermost colour itself that we actually touch, but it is not *that* that we touch and feel; we rather feel the actual hardness of the stone deep down inside it. Come now, and grasp why the image is seen   270
beyond the mirror – for it certainly seems far removed, deep down (on the other side). It is of the same kind as those things which are reliably perceived through a doorway, when the door offers an open view through itself, making many things visible outside the house; for this perception also is produced by a double, two-part air channel. First the air is perceived on this side of the   275
doors, then the doors themselves follow, to right and left, and after them the outside light brushes through the eyes together with the other air-channel and those things which are perceived in their reality outside. Thus as soon as the image of the mirror has launched itself, while on   280
its way to our eyes it shoves forward and drives on the air which is placed between itself and the eyes, making us feel all this (air) before we perceive the mirror; but when we have perceived the mirror itself also, then in exactly the same way the image which leaves our bodies reaches (the mirror), is bounced off and returns to our   285
eyes driving and rolling another air-channel in front of it, making us see this (air) before we see (the image) itself – that is how it seems to be so far removed from the mirror. These, then, are compelling reasons why there is no call for any surprise that the same thing happens to those objects seen through doorways and those objects which reflect visual images from the surface   290
of mirrors, since in both cases the phenomenon is produced by twin air-currents.

nunc ea quae nobis membrorum dextera pars est
in speculis fit ut in laeva videatur eo quod,
planitiem ad speculi veniens cum offendit imago,
non convertitur incolumis, sed recta retrorsum   295
sic eliditur, ut siquis, prius arida quam sit
cretea persona, adlidat pilaeve trabive,
atque ea continuo rectam si forte figuram
servet et elisam retro sese exprimat ipsa: (323)
fiet ut, ante oculus fuerit qui dexter, et idem   300   (324)
nunc sit laevus, et e laevo sit mutua dexter.
fit quoque de speculo in speculum ut tradatur imago,
quinque, etiam sex ut fieri simulacra suerint.
nam quaecumque retro parte interiore latebunt,
inde tamen, quamvis torte penitusque remota,   305   (329)
omnia per flexos aditus educta licebit
pluribus haec speculis videantur in aedibus esse:
usque adeo speculo in speculum translucet imago,
et cum laeva data est, fit rursum ut dextera fiat,
inde retro rursum redit et convertit eodem.   310   (334)
quin etiam quaecumque latuscula sunt speculorum
adsimili lateris flexura praedita nostri,
dextera ea propter nobis simulacra remittunt,
aut quia de speculo in speculum transfertur imago,
inde ad nos elisa bis advolat, aut etiam quod   315   (339)
circum agitur, cum venit, imago propterea quod
flexa figura docet speculi convertier ad nos.

indugredi porro pariter simulacra pedemque
ponere nobiscum credas gestumque imitari
propterea quia, de speculi qua parte recedas,   320   (344)
continuo nequeunt illinc simulacra reverti,
omnia quandoquidem cogit natura referri
ac resilire ab rebus ad aequos reddita flexus.   (347)

splendida porro oculi fugitant vitantque tueri.   (299)
sol etiam caecat, contra si tendere pergas,   325
propterea quia vis magnast ipsius et alte
aera per purum graviter simulacra feruntur
et feriunt oculos turbantia composituras.

---

298 forte *A Lambinus*: fronte *OQ*
300 et *scripsi*: ut *OQ*: ita *Lachmann*
303 sex *OQ*: aut sex *Lachmann*: sexve *Marullus*

Now the right side of our limbs in mirrors comes out
looking as if it is on the left because when the image
comes and slaps against the flat surface of the mirror it
is not turned around unharmed but is bounced straight   295
back in the way a plaster mask would, if somebody flung
one against a pillar or a beam before it was dry; if it
could possibly keep its shape unchanged the collision
would make it turn itself back to front; it will happen
that both the same eye which was formerly right is now   300
left, and the left takes the place of right in exchange. It
also happens that an image may be relayed from mirror to
mirror so that five, even six images are not unusual. For
whatever things lie hidden out of sight in the inner part
of the house, however labyrinthine it is, however deeply   305
they are secreted, can all be teased out through the maze
of passages by means of several mirrors and be seen
inside the house. So clearly does the image shine through
from mirror to mirror, and if it is offered as left it
happens in turn to become right, then in turn returns
back and reverses to the same position. But then also   310
any mirrors that have little sides curved round like our
own sides relay their images back to us right-handed for
these reasons; either because the image is carried across
from one mirror-surface to the other and only flies to us   315
after two reflections, or even because the image is spun
round on arrival, because the curved shape of the mirror
teaches it to turn round to face us.
Furthermore, you could believe that the images march
alongside us, keeping in step with us and copying our
gestures; this is because, when you move away from any   320
part of the mirror, at once the images become incapable
of being reflected from that part, since nature forces
them all to be carried back, bouncing off things and
being returned at equal angles. Furthermore, the eyes
run away from bright things and avoid looking at them.   325
The sun can even blind the eyes if you persist in
directing them towards it, because its own force is great
and also because the images are borne down heavily
through the clean air from high heaven and thus upset
the atomic structure of the eyes when they beat against
them.

praeterea splendor quicumque est acer adurit
saepe oculos ideo quod semina possidet ignis   330   (305)
multa, dolorem oculis quae gignunt insinuando.

lurida praeterea fiunt quaecumque tuentur
arquati, quia luroris de corpore eorum
semina multa fluunt simulacris obvia rerum,
multaque sunt oculis in eorum denique mixta,   335   (310)
quae contage sua palloribus omnia pingunt.

e tenebris autem quae sunt in luce tuemur
propterea quia, cum propior caliginis aer
ater init oculos prior et possedit apertos,
insequitur candens confestim lucidus aer,   340   (315)
qui quasi purgat eos ac nigras discutit umbras
aeris illius; nam multis partibus hic est
mobilior multisque minutior et mage pollens.
qui simul atque vias oculorum luce replevit
atque patefecit quas ante obsederat aer   345   (320)
ater, continuo rerum simulacra sequuntur
quae sita sunt in luce, lacessuntque ut videamus.   (322)
quod contra facere in tenebris e luce nequimus
propterea quia posterior caliginis aer
crassior insequitur, qui cuncta foramina complet   350
obsiditque vias oculorum, ne simulacra
possint ullarum rerum coniecta movere.

quadratasque procul turris cum cernimus urbis,
propterea fit uti videantur saepe rutundae,
angulus obtusus quia longe cernitur omnis,   355
sive etiam potius non cernitur ac perit eius
plaga nec ad nostras acies perlabitur ictus,
aera per multum quia dum simulacra feruntur,
cogit hebescere eum crebris offensibus aer.
hoc ubi suffugit sensum simul angulus omnis,   360
fit quasi ut ad tornum saxorum structa terantur;
non tamen ut coram quae sunt vereque rutunda,
sed quasi adumbratim paulum simulata videntur.

umbra videtur item nobis in sole moveri
et vestigia nostra sequi gestumque imitari;   365
aera si credis privatum lumine posse
indugredi, motus hominum gestumque sequentem.

---

361 terantur *Munro*: tuantur *OQ*

Besides, *any* penetrating brightness can often burn the eyes because it possesses the seeds of fire in great numbers, seeds which breed pain in the eyes as they work their way in.

Besides, everything that jaundiced people look at turns yellow, because the seeds of yellowness flow in great numbers from their body and meet the images of things, and then also because there are many such seeds mixed in their eyes which paint everything monochrome yellow in their infectious contact with them.

Yet we see things that are in the light when we are in the dark for this reason: the black air of darkness is closer and so first to enter the open eyes and take possession of them; then follows at once the white air of light which, as it were, cleans them out and scatters the black shadows of that first air – for this second air is many times more mobile, many times more finely-textured and more powerful. As soon as this air has filled the passages of the eyes again with light and opened those roads which the black air had previously blockaded, at once the images of things which are in the light follow up and incite us to see them. Conversely, however, we cannot do this with regard to objects in the dark when we are in the light, because the thicker air of darkness follows on behind (the other air), fills up all the apertures, blockades the passages of the eyes and thus renders the images flung at them incapable of arousing sensation. When we see the square towers of a city from far off, it often happens that they seem round, because all angles look blunted when seen from a distance or rather are not even seen at all, the force of the blow is dissipated, nor does the impact complete its gliding way to our eyes, because the air compels the images to lose their sharpness by frequent collisions on their long journey through a great mass of air.

When by this means every angle at once has escaped our sense, the structures of stone happen to look as if they are rounded on a lathe – without looking exactly like stones that are really round seen close to, they still seem, to a small extent, like shadowy copies of these.

Again, our shadow seems to move in the sunlight, to follow our tracks and imitate our gestures, if you believe that air devoid of light can march following movements and gestures of human beings. For that which we usually

330

335

340

345

350

355

360

365

31

nam nil esse potest aliud nisi lumine cassus
aer id quod nos umbram perhibere suemus.
nimirum quia terra locis ex ordine certis   370
lumine privatur solis quacumque meantes
officimus, repletur item quod liquimus eius,
propterea fit uti videatur, quae fuit umbra
corporis, e regione eadem nos usque secuta.
semper enim nova se radiorum lumina fundunt   375
primaque dispereunt, quasi in ignem lana trahatur.
propterea facile et spoliatur lumine terra
et repletur item nigrasque sibi abluit umbras.

nec tamen hic oculos falli concedimus hilum.
nam quocumque loco sit lux atque umbra tueri   380
illorum est; eadem vero sint lumina necne,
umbraque quae fuit hic eadem nunc transeat illuc,
an potius fiat paulo quod diximus ante,
hoc animi demum ratio discernere debet,
nec possunt oculi naturam noscere rerum.   385
proinde animi vitium hoc oculis adfingere noli.

qua vehimur navi, fertur, cum stare videtur;
quae manet in statione, ea praeter creditur ire.
et fugere ad puppim colles campique videntur
quos agimus praeter navem velisque volamus.   390

sidera cessare aetheriis adfixa cavernis
cuncta videntur, et adsiduo sunt omnia motu,
quandoquidem longos obitus exorta revisunt,
cum permensa suo sunt caelum corpore claro.
solque pari ratione manere et luna videtur   395
in statione, ea quae ferri res indicat ipsa.
exstantisque procul medio de gurgite montis
classibus inter quos liber patet exitus ingens,
insula coniunctis tamen ex his una videtur.

atria versari et circumcursare columnae   400
usque adeo fit uti pueris videantur, ubi ipsi
desierunt verti, vix ut iam credere possint
non supra sese ruere omnia tecta minari.

iamque rubrum tremulis iubar ignibus erigere alte
cum coeptat natura supraque extollere montes,   405

32

call our shadow can be nothing other than air that is lacking in light. This is no doubt because the earth is deprived of sunlight in fixed, specific places in succession, depending on where we block the light as we move; when we have left a place it is filled up again, which makes it seem that that which has been the body's shadow in the past is one and the same which has followed us constantly in a straight line. For new rays of light are always pouring forth and the first ones perishing, like wool being drawn into the fire. Thus the earth is easily robbed of its light and filled again as it washes away the black shadows.

Yet we do not grant that the eyes are deceived in any way in all this. For it is their function to see the places where light and shadow are; but whether the light is the same or different, whether the shadow which was here is the same as the one which is now going there or whether it is rather a case of that which we mentioned before; these are distinctions which must be decided by the reasoning power of the mind, and that alone, as eyes cannot apprehend the nature of things. Do not then arraign the eyes with what is a fault of the mind.

The ship we are sailing in moves but seems to stand still, while the one that is lying at anchor is believed to be passing us by. Hills and plains seem to fly towards the stern when we drive the ship past them, flying with our sails.

The stars all appear motionless, fastened to the caverns of the upper air, and yet they are all moving constantly since they rise and go back to their setting points afar off when they have paced out the sky with their bright body. Similarly the sun and the moon seem to remain in their position, and yet the facts prove that they move. Mountains towering up far off out of the middle of the sea may have a massive channel in between them affording freedom of exit to whole fleets, yet they appear to be joined together to form a single island.

Halls seem to rotate, columns seem to whirl around when children have just stopped spinning round – so much so that they can hardly believe that the whole building is not threatening to crash down upon them. And then, when Nature starts to raise up on high her red shaft of

370

375

380

385

390

395

400

405

quos ibi tum supra sol montis esse videtur
comminus ipse suo contingens fervidus igni,
vix absunt nobis missus bis mille sagittae,
vix etiam cursus quingentos saepe veruti;
inter eos solemque iacent immania ponti   410
aequora substrata aetheriis ingentibus oris,
interiectaque sunt terrarum milia multa
quae variae retinent gentes et saecla ferarum.

at conlectus aquae digitum non altior unum,
qui lapides inter sistit per strata viarum,   415
despectum praebet sub terras impete tanto,
a terris quantum caeli patet altus hiatus,
nubila despicere et caelum ut videare videre, et
corpora mirande sub terras abdita caelo.
denique ubi in medio nobis equus acer obhaesit   420
flumine et in rapidas amnis despeximus undas,
stantis equi corpus transversum ferre videtur
vis et in adversum flumen contrudere raptim,
et, quocumque oculos traiecimus, omnia ferri
et fluere adsimili nobis ratione videntur.   425

porticus aequali quamvis est denique ductu
stansque in perpetuum paribus suffulta columnis,
longa tamen parte ab summa cum tota videtur,
paulatim trahit angusti fastigia coni,
tecta solo iungens atque omnia dextera laevis,   430
donec in obscurum coni conduxit acumen.

in pelago nautis ex undis ortus in undis
sol fit uti videatur obire et condere lumen,
quippe ubi nil aliud nisi aquam caelumque tuentur;
ne leviter credas labefactari undique sensus.   435

at maris ignaris in portu clauda videntur
navigia aplustris fractis obnitier undis.
nam quaecumque supra rorem salis edita pars est
remorum, recta est, et recta superne guberna;
quae demersa liquore obeunt, refracta videntur   440
omnia converti sursumque supina reverti
et reflexa prope in summo fluitare liquore.

406 ibi *ed. Juntina*: ubi *OQ*: tıbi *Naugerius*
414 conlectus *Lambinus*: coniectus *OQ*
418 videre et *Lambinus*: videre *OQ*
437 undis *F*: undas *OQ*: undae *Lachmann*
440 liquore *OQ*: liquorem *Lachmann*

light with quivering fires, and to lift it clear above the
mountains, it is then and there that the sun seems to be
above the mountains, red-hot and touching them at close
quarters with his fire. The mountains are barely two
thousand bowshots away from us, barely even five
hundred flights of a javelin on many occasions; yet
between them and the sun lie the immensities of the sea   410
laid out flat below the massive shores of the upper air,
as well as the many thousands of lands cast in between
them, occupied by different races of men and species of
animal.
Yet a puddle of water no deeper than a single finger's
breadth which collects between the stones in paved   415
streets affords a view down below the earth of a depth
proportional to the height of the yawning heavens from
the earth, so that you seem to look down on the clouds
and the sky and see bodies hidden marvellously under the
earth in the sky.
Then when our spirited horse sticks in midstream and we   420
look down into the swirling waters of the river, although
the horse is standing still it looks as though the current
is carrying it sideways and thrusting it hard upstream,
and wherever we turn our eyes everything seems to be
carried along flowing in the same direction as ourselves.   425
Then, a colonnade may be built on straight lines and
stand supported by pillars that are equal throughout, yet
when the whole length is seen from one end it gradually
draws together into the point of a narrow cone, joining
up the roof to the floor, the entire right side to that on   430
the left, until it joins them all together into the point of
a cone which cannot be seen.
To sailors on the sea, the sun seems to rise out of the
waves and then to set and sink its light in the waves,
since they see nothing other than water and sky; (I tell
you this) to stop you thinking foolishly that the senses
are being undermined on all sides.   435
To those ignorant of the sea, ships in port seem crippled
with their poops broken as they ride against the waves;
for whatever part of the oars is raised up above the dew
of the brine is straight, and the upper part of the
rudder is straight; but those things which sink plunged
in water all seem refracted, slewed round, twisted round   440
flat face upwards and bent so as virtually to be floating
on the water's surface.

raraque per caelum cum venti nubila portant
tempore nocturno, tum splendida signa videntur
labier adversum nimbos atque ire superne   445
longe aliam in partem ac vera ratione feruntur.

at si forte oculo manus uni subdita subter
pressit eum, quodam sensu fit uti videantur
omnia quae tuimur fieri tum bina tuendo,
bina lucernarum florentia lumina flammis   450
binaque per totas aedis geminare supellex
et duplicis hominum facies et corpora bina.
denique cum suavi devinxit membra sopore
somnus, et in summa corpus iacet omne quiete,
tum vigilare tamen nobis et membra movere   455
nostra videmur, et in noctis caligine caeca
cernere censemus solem lumenque diurnum,
conclusoque loco caelum mare flumina montis
mutare et campos pedibus transire videmur,
et sonitus audire, severa silentia noctis   460
undique cum constent, et reddere dicta tacentes.
cetera de genere hoc mirande multa videmus,
quae violare fidem quasi sensibus omnia quaerunt;
nequiquam, quoniam pars horum maxima fallit
propter opinatus animi quos addimus ipsi,   465
pro visis ut sint quae non sunt sensibu' visa.
nam nil aegrius est quam res secernere apertas
ab dubiis, animus quas ab se protinus addit.
denique nil sciri siquis putat, id quoque nescit
an sciri possit, quoniam nil scire fatetur.   470
hunc igitur contra mittam contendere causam,
qui capite ipse sua in statuit vestigia sese.
et tamen hoc quoque uti concedam scire, at id ipsum
quaeram, cum in rebus veri nil viderit ante,
unde sciat quid sit scire et nescire vicissim,   475
notitiam veri quae res falsique crearit,
et dubium certo quae res differre probarit.
invenies primis ab sensibus esse creatam
notitiem veri neque sensus posse refelli.

---

472 sua *Lachmann*: suo *OQ*
479 sensus *Marullus*: sensu *OQ*

When the winds carry scattered clouds through the sky at night time, the brilliant stars seem to glide up against the clouds and move on high in a direction very different 445 from their true course.

Then, if a hand is applied from underneath up to one eye, and presses it, it happens by some quirk of sensation that everything we look at becomes double with the looking, double lamp-lights flowering with flame, twin 450 furniture multiplying all over the house, men with two faces and double bodies.

Then, when sleep has fettered our limbs in pleasing repose and the entire body lies in total rest, we nonetheless seem to ourselves to be awake and to be 455 moving our limbs, and in the blind blackness of night we think we see the sun and the light of day, we think we can exchange our confined space for sky, sea, rivers, mountains, we seem to be crossing plains on foot and hearing sounds when the strict silences of night are 460 firmly entrenched all around, we seem to be uttering words when we are silent.

There are many other things of this kind which we see in amazement, all of which are seeking, as it were, to undermine our trust in the senses, in vain; for the majority of these only deceive us because of the mental preconceptions which we supply ourselves, so that things 465 rank as genuine perceptions when they have not actually been seen by the senses at all. For there is nothing harder than to distinguish between the plain facts and the dubious judgements which the mind itself readily supplies.

Then again, anyone who thinks that nothing is known is also incapable of knowing whether his ignorance is known either, since he admits to knowing nothing. I shall 470 therefore refrain from pleading my case against this man, who has taken up a position with his own footprints on his head.

Yet were I to grant that he does know his own ignorance, I would still press this very question: how does he know what knowledge and ignorance respectively *are*, since he 475 has never seen anything true in the material world? What then has given him the concept of 'truth' and 'falsehood', and what has demonstrated to him that the doubtful is not the same as the certain? You will find that the concept of truth has been formed primarily from the senses, and that the senses cannot be refuted. For something of

37

nam maiore fide debet reperirier illud,   480
sponte sua veris quod possit vincere falsa.
quid maiore fide porro quam sensus haberi
debet? an ab sensu falso ratio orta valebit
dicere eos contra, quae tota ab sensibus orta est?
qui nisi sunt veri, ratio quoque falsa fit omnis.   485

an poterunt oculos aures reprehendere, an aures
tactus? an hunc porro tactum sapor arguet oris,
an confutabunt nares oculive revincent?
non, ut opinor, ita est. nam seorsum cuique potestas
divisast, sua vis cuiquest, ideoque necesse est   490
et quod molle sit et gelidum fervensque seorsum
et seorsum varios rerum sentire colores
et quaecumque coloribu' sint coniuncta videre.
seorsus item sapor oris habet vim, seorsus odores
nascuntur, sorsum sonitus. ideoque necesse est   495
non possint alios alii convincere sensus.
nec porro poterunt ipsi reprehendere sese,
aequa fides quoniam debebit semper haberi.
proinde quod in quoquest his visum tempore, verumst.
et si non poterit ratio dissolvere causam,   500
cur ea quae fuerint iuxtim quadrata, procul sint
visa rutunda, tamen praestat rationis egentem
reddere mendose causas utriusque figurae,
quam manibus manifesta suis emittere quoquam
et violare fidem primam et convellere tota   505
fundamenta quibus nixatur vita salusque.
non modo enim ratio ruat omnis, vita quoque ipsa
concidat extemplo, nisi credere sensibus ausis
praecipitisque locos vitare et cetera quae sint
in genere hoc fugienda, sequi contraria quae sint.   510
illa tibi est igitur verborum copia cassa
omnis, quae contra sensus instructa paratast.
denique ut in fabrica, si pravast regula prima,
normaque si fallax rectis regionibus exit,
et libella aliqua si ex parti claudicat hilum,   515
omnia mendose fieri atque obstipa necesse est
prava cubantia prona supina atque absona tecta,

---

491 seorsum *Bentley*: videri *OQ*

greater reliability must be discovered, to do so, 480
something which could independently conquer the false
with the true. Then what is there which is incontestably
more reliable than the senses? Will reason, sprung from
mendacious sense-perception, have the power to
contradict the senses when it is wholly derived from
them? If the senses are not true, then all reason is also 485
rendered false. Or will the ears be able to upbraid the
eyes, or touch judge the ears? Or will taste in the mouth
refute this sense of touch, the nostrils silence it, the
eyes subdue it? I think not. For each sense has its own
capability peculiar to itself and its own distinctive power; 490
it is thus necessary to perceive softness, icy cold and
burning heat with sensation quite distinct from that with
which we must feel the different colours of things and see
whatever things are joined up with the colours. Hence
also the taste of the mouth has its own distinctive power,
smells are created in a manner peculiar to themselves, as 495
are sounds. It is therefore quite impossible that these
senses should be able to refute one another; furthermore,
they will not be able to criticise themselves either, since
their reliability must be consistently maintained at all
times. It follows, then, that anything which has been
seen by these senses at any time is true.
If reason proves incapable of disentangling the reason 500
whereby things which were square when seen close to
look round from a distance, it is still preferable to render
explanations for the two shapes untruthfully through lack
of reason rather than at any point to let the clearly
graspable slip from our grasp and thus to break faith at
the most basic level and to tear up the entire foundations 505
on which our life and safety depend. For not only would
all reasoning collapse, life itself would also fall to pieces
at once if you didn't have the courage to believe your
senses, avoiding precipitous places and other undesirable 510
things of this kind, seeking the opposite. So, I tell you,
all that plethora of words which has been drawn up and
marshalled against the senses is a waste of breath.
Finally as in a building, if the original ruler is not
straight, if the square is not true but deviates from the
right angle, if the plumb line limps askew at all in any 515
direction, then the whole house must be built wrong,
crooked bulging leaning forwards, leaning backwards and
all out of proportion, so that some parts of it look as if

iam ruere ut quaedam videantur velle, ruantque,
prodita iudiciis fallacibus omnia primis,
sic igitur ratio tibi rerum prava necessest   520
falsaque sit, falsis quaecumque ab sensibus ortast.

nunc alii sensus quo pacto quisque suam rem
sentiat, haudquaquam ratio scruposa relicta est.

principio auditur sonus et vox omnis, in auris
insinuata suo pepulere ubi corpore sensum.   525
corpoream quoque enim vocem constare fatendumst
et sonitum, quoniam possunt inpellere sensus.
praeterea radit vox fauces saepe, facitque
asperiora foras gradiens arteria clamor,
quippe per angustum turba maiore coorta   530
ire foras ubi coeperunt primordia vocum,
scilicet expletis quoque ianua raditur oris.
haud igitur dubiumst quin voces verbaque constent
corporeis e principiis, ut laedere possint.
nec te fallit item quid corporis auferat et quid   535
detrahat ex hominum nervis ac viribus ipsis
perpetuus sermo nigrai noctis ad umbram
aurorae perductus ab exoriente nitore,
praesertim si cum summost clamore profusus.
ergo corpoream vocem constare necessest,   540
multa loquens quoniam amittit de corpore partem.
asperitas autem vocis fit ab asperitate   (551)
principiorum, et item levor levore creatur.   (552)
nec simili penetrant auris primordia forma,
cum tuba depresso graviter sub murmure mugit   545
et reboat raucum buxus cita barbara bombum,
et gelida volucres nocte hortis e fruticosis
cum liquidam tollunt lugubri voce querellam.

hasce igitur penitus voces cum corpore nostro
exprimimus rectoque foras emittimus ore,   550

---

532 expletis *OQ*: expleti *Lachmann*
542–3 (551–2) *huc transposuit Lambinus*
546 buxus cita *Büchner*: retro cita *OQ*: Berecyntia
Vossius: regio cita *Lachmann*
547 gelida volucres nocte hortis e fruticosis *Richter*:
validis necti tortis ex Heliconis *OQ*: et convallibu' cycni
intortis *M.F. Smith: alii alia*

they want to fall down at once, and some parts do
actually fall, all of it betrayed by the original judgements
which were not true; in just this way, therefore, any   520
reasoning about material things must also be crooked and
false if it is derived from senses that are false.
Now it is left to us to explain how each of the other
senses perceives its own object – a line of argument that
is by no means jagged underfoot.
In the first place all sounds and voices are heard when
they have worked their way into the ears and then struck   525
upon the sense with their body. For voice and sound are
incontestably material in composition, since they can beat
against the senses. Besides, the voice often scrapes the
throat and shouting makes the windpipe rougher as it
makes it way out. For when the voice atoms form an   530
excessively large crowd and begin to come out through
the narrow space, then obviously the doorway of the
mouth is also scraped with the windpipe fully congested.
Hence, as they can injure the body, there can be no
doubt that voices and words are made up from physical   535
particles. Again, you must be aware how much continuous
talking drains men's bodies, sapping their very sinews
and strength, when they talk non-stop from the rising
gleam of dawn right up to the shadow of black night,
especially if the speech is poured forth at full volume.
Therefore the voice must be physical, since the man who   540
speaks a lot loses part of his body.
Roughness of the voice is due to the roughness of the
particles, as in the same way smoothness of the voice
is produced by their smoothness. The elements that
pierce the ears are of quite different shapes when the   545
trumpet lows with a deep base boom and the boxwood
pipe, the virtuoso foreign instrument, re-echoes its
hoarse roar, and when in the icy chill of night the birds
raise their melodious dirge with mournful voice from the
shrubbery of the gardens.
So when we squeeze these voices out from deep down in   550
our body and shoot them straight out of the mouth, the

41

mobilis articulat verborum daedala lingua
formaturaque labrorum pro parte figurat.   (550)
hoc ubi non longum spatiumst unde illa profecta
perveniat vox quaeque, necessest verba quoque ipsa
plane exaudiri discernique articulatim;   555
servat enim formaturam servatque figuram.
at si interpositum spatium sit longius aequo,
aera per multum confundi verba necessest
et conturbari vocem, dum transvolat auras.
ergo fit sonitum ut possis sentire neque illam   560
internoscere, verborum sententia quae sit:
usque adeo confusa venit vox inque pedita.
praeterea verbum saepe unum perciet auris
omnibus in populo, missum praeconis ab ore.
in multas igitur voces vox una repente   565
diffugit, in privas quoniam se dividit auris,
obsignans formam verbis clarumque sonorem.
at quae pars vocum non auris incidit ipsas,
praeterlata perit frustra diffusa per auras;
pars, solidis adlisa locis, reiecta sonorem   570
reddit et interdum frustratur imagine verbi.
quae bene cum videas, rationem reddere possis
tute tibi atque aliis, quo pacto per loca sola
saxa paris formas verborum ex ordine reddant,
palantis comites cum montis inter opacos   575
quaerimus et magna dispersos voce ciemus.
sex etiam aut septem loca vidi reddere voces,
unam cum iaceres: ita colles collibus ipsi
verba repulsantes iterabant docta referri.
haec loca capripedes satyros nymphasque tenere   580
finitimi fingunt, et faunos esse loquuntur,
quorum noctivago strepitu ludoque iocanti
adfirmant volgo taciturna silentia rumpi,
chordarumque sonos fieri dulcisque querellas,
tibia quas fundit digitis pulsata canentum,   585
et genus agricolum late sentiscere, cum Pan,
pinea semiferi capitis velamina quassans,
unco saepe labro calamos percurrit hiantis,
fistula silvestrem ne cesset fundere musam.
cetera de genere hoc monstra ac portenta loquuntur,   590

---

553 illa *OQ*: una *Bentley*
579 docta referri *Lachmann*: dicta referri *OQ*: referre
Marullus

flexible crafty tongue, fashioner of words, saws them into
sections and then the shaping of the lips performs its
function of moulding them. Now when it is no long race
that each of those voices has to run from its starting
point to reach us, then the separate words must be   555
clearly heard and sifted out joint by joint; for the sound
preserves its shaping and its form. But if the intervening
course is unreasonably long the words must be mixed up
in their passage through a good deal of air, the voice
must be distorted while it is flying through the breezes.
Thus it happens that you can feel the sound but still be   560
unable to discern the meaning of the words – so mixed
up, so encumbered is the voice that arrives. Besides,
often a single word thrown from the mouth of a crier
stirs the ears of everybody in a public assembly.
Therefore a single voice suddenly disintegrates into many   565
voices while in flight, since it shares itself out into
separate ears, stamping a shape and a clear sound on the
words. But those voices which do not fall into the ears
themselves continue travelling past and come to nothing,
dispersed idly through the breezes. Some of them are   570
flung at hard surfaces and bounce back, reflecting the
sound and sometimes deluding us with the copy of a
word. When you see this clearly, you could explain to
yourself and to others how in lonely regions rocks reflect
the exact shapes of words in the correct sequence, when
we are searching among the lightless mountains for our   575
straying companions scattered afar, calling them at the
top of our voices. I have even seen places return six or
seven voices when you only fired one yourself – this is
how hills bounce words to hills of their own accord,
repeating to themselves the words that are trained to
come back. Local people imagine that goat-footed satyrs   580
and nymphs haunt these places, and say that there are
fauns, by whose night-roaming noise and playful pranks
they commonly claim the speechless silences are broken as
the sounds of stringed instruments arise, and the sweet
sad music which the pipe pours out when it is struck by   585
the players' fingers; farming folk, they say, become
aware of Pan from miles away, as he tosses the pine
coverings of his half-bestial head, often running the full
length of his open reeds with his hooked lip to keep the
pipe pouring out an unbroken stream of woodland music.   590
They also talk of all the other marvellous and prodigious

43

ne loca deserta ab divis quoque forte putentur
sola tenere. ideo iactant miracula dictis
aut aliqua ratione alia ducuntur, ut omne
humanum genus est avidum nimis auricularum.

quod superest, non est mirandum qua ratione,   595
per loca quae nequeunt oculi res cernere apertas,
haec loca per voces veniant aurisque lacessant.
conloquium clausis foribus quoque saepe videmus,
nimirum quia vox per flexa foramina rerum
incolumis transire potest, simulacra renutant;   600
perscinduntur enim, nisi recta foramina tranant,
qualia sunt vitri, species qua travolat omnis.
praeterea partis in cunctas dividitur vox,
ex aliis aliae quoniam gignuntur, ubi una
dissiluit semel in multas exorta, quasi ignis   605
saepe solet scintilla suos se spargere in ignis.
ergo replentur loca vocibus abdita retro
omnia quae circum fervunt sonituque cientur.
at simulacra viis derectis omnia tendunt
ut sunt missa semel; quapropter cernere nemo   610
saepe supra potis est, at voces accipere extra.
et tamen ipsa quoque haec, dum transit clausa domorum,
vox obtunditur atque auris confusa penetrat
et sonitum potius quam verba audire videmur.

nec, qui sentimus sucum, lingua atque palatum   615
plusculum habent in se rationis plusve operai.
principio sucum sentimus in ore, cibum cum
mandendo exprimimus, ceu plenam spongiam aquai
siquis forte manu premere ac siccare coepit.
inde quod exprimimus per caulas omne palati   620
diditur et rarae per flexa foramina linguae.
hoc ubi levia sunt manantis corpora suci,
suaviter attingunt et suaviter omnia tractant
umida linguai circum sudantia templa.
at contra pungunt sensum lacerantque coorta,   625
quanto quaeque magis sunt asperitate repleta.
deinde voluptas est e suco fine palati;

---

611 saepe *OQ*: saepta *Wakefield*:
615 nec *Marullus*: hoc *OQ*
616 plusve operai *scripsi*: plus opere *OQ*: plus operaeve
Lachmann

things of this kind, just in case they are thought to haunt a region that is so deserted that even the gods have left it. Either that is the reason why they boast of these wonderful things, or they have some other motive, as the human race is marked by excessively greedy little ears.

Next, there is no mystery about how voices can pass through places through which the eyes cannot see clearly, and stimulate the ears. We are often aware of a conversation going on even behind closed doors, obviously because voice can pass unscathed through the labyrinthine passages of things, but images refuse. For they are cut to pieces if they are not swimming through straight passages such as those of glass, which any appearance can fly through. Besides, the voice is shared out in all directions because the sounds give birth to other sounds when what came out as a single utterance has sprung apart into many, just as a spark of fire often spreads itself out into fires of its own.

That is why places hidden well away from sight are filled with voices and all around they boil and thrill with sound. Visual images all move forward in straight lines once they have been discharged, which is why nobody can see over the hedge and yet sounds are audible outside. Yet even a voice is blunted on its passage through the confined parts of the house and pierces the ears in a distorted state, and we seem to hear a sound rather than words.

Nor does it require the tiniest extra thought or work to explain the tongue and the palate, and how we feel taste. In the first place we feel taste in the mouth when we squeeze food in chewing it, as if somebody were to squeeze a sponge full of water with his hand and begin to dry it. Then that which we squeeze out is all spread out through the pores of the palate and through the tortuous passages of the absorbent tongue.

So, when the particles of seeping juice are smooth, they sweetly touch, they sweetly massage all the moist, sweating regions of the tongue all around. On the other hand, the particles sting the sense and tear it apart in their attack, the more they are individually filled with roughness. Next, pleasure derived from taste is confined

595

600

605

610

615

620

625

45

cum vero deorsum per fauces praecipitavit,
nulla voluptas est, dum diditur omnis in artus.
nec refert quicquam quo victu corpus alatur,   630
dummodo quod capias concoctum didere possis
artubus et stomachi validum servare tenorem.
nunc aliis alius qui sit cibus ut videamus
expediam, quareve, aliis quod triste et amarumst,
hoc tamen esse aliis possit perdulce videri.   635
tantaque in his rebus distantia differitasque est
ut quod aliis cibus est aliis fuat acre venenum.
est itaque et serpens, hominis quae tacta salivis
disperit ac sese mandendo conficit ipsa.
praeterea nobis veratrum est acre venenum,   640
at capris adipes et cocturnicibus auget.
id quibus ut fiat rebus cognoscere possis,
principio meminisse decet quae diximus ante,
semina multimodis in rebus mixta teneri.
porro omnes quaecumque cibum capiunt animantes,   645
ut sunt dissimiles extrinsecus et generatim
extima membrorum circumcaesura coercet,
proinde et seminibus constant variante figura.
semina cum porro distent, differre necessest
intervalla viasque, foramina quae perhibemus,   650
omnibus in membris et in ore ipsoque palato.
esse minora igitur quaedam maioraque debent,
esse triquetra aliis, aliis quadrata necessest,
multa rutunda, modis multis multangula quaedam.
namque figurarum ratio ut motusque reposcunt,   655
proinde foraminibus debent differre figurae,
et variare viae proinde ac textura coercet.
hoc ubi quod suave est aliis aliis fit amarum,
illi, cui suave est, levissima corpora debent
contractabiliter caulas intrare palati,   660
at contra quibus est eadem res intus acerba,
aspera nimirum penetrant hamataque fauces.
nunc facile est ex his rebus cognoscere quaeque.
quippe ubi cui febris bili superante coorta est
aut alia ratione aliquast vis excita morbi,   665

---

632 validum *Orth*: umidum *OQ*: umidulum *Lachmann*
633 ut videamus *OQ*: atque venenum *Bailey*: *alii alia*
638 est itaque et *N.P. Howard*: est itaque ut *OQ*:
pestifera ut *Richter*
648 variante figura *Lachmann*: variantque *OQ*

to the palate; when it has plunged down through the throat there is no pleasure, while it is all being divided up into the limbs.
Nor does it matter at all what food is used to nourish the body, as long as what you take is digestible and you can spread it out to the limbs and maintain the sturdy condition of the stomach. Now I shall explain how it is that different creatures have different food, for us to see the reason for this, and why it is that what is sour and bitter to some can yet seem delicious to others. There is so much difference and variety in these matters that what is food to some can be virulent poison to others. There is thus even a snake which, when touched by human saliva, perishes and masticates itself to death. Besides, Hellebore is a vicious poison to us, but makes goats and quails fat. To be able to understand how this happens, you should first of all remember what we said earlier, that the seeds contained in things are mixed in many different ways. Furthermore, just as all animals that consume food are outwardly unlike each other, and as the external contour of their limbs bars them off species by species, accordingly they are composed of seeds of widely differing shape. Furthermore, since the seeds are different, the gaps and passages – which we call channels – must also be different in all the limbs, including the mouth and palate itself. Therefore some must be smaller, some larger, some creatures must have triangular seeds, others square, many must be round, some must have a wide variety of polygonal seeds. For as the arrangement of shapes and their movements demand, so must the channels differ in shape and the passages vary according to the limitations of the atomic texture. Thus what is pleasant to some is bitter to others in those cases when the creature which finds things sweet must have very smooth bodies entering the pores of his palate caressingly, while those who find the same thing bitter inside surely have rough and hooked bodies piercing their throat. From the above expanation it is easy to understand every single case. For when bile gets the upper hand and fever has afflicted a man or when the force of disease in some form

630

635

640

645

650

655

660

665

perturbatur ibi iam totum corpus, et omnes
commutantur ibi positurae principiorum;
fit prius ad sensum ut quae corpora conveniebant
nunc non conveniant, et cetera sint magis apta,
quae penetrata queunt sensum progignere acerbum;   670
utraque enim sunt in mellis commixta sapore,
id quod iam supera tibi saepe ostendimus ante.

nunc age, quo pacto naris adiectus odoris
tangat agam. primum res multas esse necessest
unde fluens volvat varius se fluctus odorum,   675
et fluere et mitti volgo spargique putandumst;
verum aliis alius magis est animantibus aptus
dissimilis propter formas. ideoque per auras
mellis apes quamvis longe ducuntur odore,
volturiique cadaveribus. tum fissa ferarum   680
ungula quo tulerit gressum promissa canum vis
ducit, et humanum longe praesentit odorem
Romulidarum arcis servator, candidus anser.
sic aliis alius nidor datus ad sua quemque
pabula ducit et a taetro resilire veneno   685
cogit, eoque modo servantur saecla ferarum.
hic odor ipse igitur, naris quicumque lacessit,
est alio ut possit permitti longius alter;
sed tamen haud quisquam tam longe fertur eorum
quam sonitus, quam vox, mitto iam dicere quam res   690
quae feriunt oculorum acies visumque lacessunt.
errabundus enim tarde venit ac perit ante,
paulatim facilis distractus in aeris auras,
ex alto primum quia vix emittitur ex re:
nam penitus fluere atque recedere rebus odores   695
significat quod fracta magis redolere videntur
omnia, quod contrita, quod igni conlabefacta:
deinde videre licet maioribus esse creatum
principiis quam vox, quoniam per saxea saepta
non penetrat, qua vox volgo sonitusque feruntur.   700
quare etiam quod olet non tam facile esse videbis
investigare in qua sit regione locatum;
refrigescit enim cunctando plaga per auras,
nec calida ad sensum decurrit nuntia rerum.

---

704 decurrit *Lambinus*: decurrunt *OQ*

has been aroused in him in a different way, then the
whole body is thrown into disorder and the positions of
the elements are all changed; it then happens that the
bodies which used to be suitable to cause sensation are
no longer suitable and others are now more fitted for the
task, being able to pierce through and produce a bitter   670
sensation; for both types of body are mixed together
in the   taste of   honey - a fact which I have often
demonstrated to you in the past.
Come now, I will explain how the impact of smell touches
the nostrils. Firstly there must be many things from
which a flowing stream of smells of all kinds rolls, smells   675
that are to be thought of as flowing, being discharged
and being spread all over. But each particular smell is
more suited to some animals than to others, on account of
their differing shapes. Thus bees, however far away they
are, are drawn through the breezes by the smell of   680
honey, vultures by corpses. Then the force of hounds
sent on ahead leads us to wherever the cloven hoof of
wild beasts has brought its track, and the white goose,
guardian of the citadel of the sons of Romulus, senses
the smell of man from afar off. Thus different creatures
are given different smells which lead each one to its own   685
food and force them to shy away from foul poison; this is
how the species of wild beasts are kept alive.
Now as for this smell itself - any smell that strikes the
nostrils - it is clear that one smell could carry further
than another; but none of them travels as far as sound,   690
as voice, not to mention the things which strike the
eyesight and provoke vision. For a smell is likely to lose
its way and arrive late, and dies too soon, having no
strength to resist gradual disintegration into the breezes
of the air, firstly because as it comes from deep down it
is only discharged with difficulty; and the fact that all   695
things have a stronger smell when they are broken,
crushed or made to collapse in fire is evidence that smells
in leaving things flow from deep inside.
Next it may be seen that a smell is made up of larger
elements than voice, since it does not penetrate stone
walls, yet voice and sound commonly travel thus. For this   700
reason you will also see how it is not so easy to track
down the exact location of a smell; for the impact grows
cold in its dilatory course through the breezes, nor does
it run hot-footed to the sense with news of the material

errant saepe canes itaque et vestigia quaerunt.   705
nec tamen hoc solis in odoribus atque saporum
in generest, sed item species rerum atque colores
non ita conveniunt ad sensus omnibus omnes,
ut non sint aliis quaedam magis acria visu.
quin etiam gallum, noctem explaudentibus alis   710
auroram clara consuetum voce vocare,
noenu queunt rabidi contra constare leones
inque tueri: ita continuo meminere fugai,
nimirum quia sunt gallorum in corpore quaedam
semina, quae cum sunt oculis inmissa leonum,   715
pupillas interfodiunt acremque dolorem
praebent, ut nequeant contra durare feroces;
cum tamen haec nostras acies nil laedere possint,
aut quia non penetrant aut quod penetrantibus illis
exitus ex oculis liber datur, in remorando   720
laedere ne possint ex ulla lumina parte.
nunc age, quae moveant animum res accipe, et unde
quae veniunt veniant in mentem percipe paucis.
principio hoc dico, rerum simulacra vagari
multa modis multis in cunctas undique partis   725
tenvia, quae facile inter se iunguntur in auris,
obvia cum veniunt, ut aranea bratteaque auri.
quippe etenim multo magis haec sunt tenvia textu
quam quae percipiunt oculos visumque lacessunt,
corporis haec quoniam penetrant per rara cientque   730
tenvem animi naturam intus sensumque lacessunt.
Centauros itaque et Scyllarum membra videmus
Cerbereasque canum facies simulacraque eorum
quorum morte obita tellus amplectitur ossa,
omne genus quoniam passim simulacra feruntur,   735
partim sponte sua quae fiunt aere in ipso,
partim quae variis ab rebus cumque recedunt
et quae confiunt ex horum facta figuris.
nam certe ex vivo Centauri non fit imago,
nulla fuit quoniam talis natura animalis;   740
verum ubi equi atque hominis casu convenit imago,
haerescit facile extemplo, quod diximus ante,
propter subtilem naturam et tenvia texta.
cetera de genere hoc eadem ratione creantur.

---

712 rabidi *Wakefield*: rapidi *OQ*
740 animalis *Lambinus*: anima *OQ*: animantis *Gifanius*

objects. That is why dogs often go off course and search   705
for tracks.
Nor is this so only in the case of smells and tastes, but
similarly the appearance and colours of things do not all
fit everyone's senses so well that there are not some
things that are sharper on the eyes for some creatures.   710
Indeed the cock, whose wings applaud the night away and
who habitually summons the dawn with his clear voice, is
a beast which ravening lions find it impossible to stand
up to and stare at. They immediately turn their thoughts
to escape, presumably because there are some seeds in
the body of cocks which, when injected into the eyes of   715
lions, bore right into the pupils and cause piercing pain,
so that for all their ferocity they cannot withstand them.
Yet these seeds cannot hurt our eyes at all, either
because they do not penetrate, or because if they do
penetrate they are granted a free passage from the eyes   720
to prevent them hurting the eyes in any part by
lingering there.
Come now, hear what things stir the mind, and grasp in
a few words the origin of those things that come into the
mind. First of all I declare that images of things are
roaming everywhere in all directions in great numbers and   725
in a great many ways, images that are thin and easily
join together in the air when they collide, being like
spider's web or gold leaf. For indeed these images are
much finer in texture than those which take over the   730
eyes and stimulate vision, since they pierce through the
pores of the body and bestir the insubstantial matter of
the mind and stimulate sensation. Thus it is that we see
Centaurs and the limbs of Scyllas, Cerberean faces of
dogs and the images of those who have met their death,
whose bones the earth embraces – this is because images   735
of every type are moving everywhere, some images
materialising spontaneously in the air itself, others
peeling off a wide variety of objects, others made from
the shapes of these images merged together into composite
images. For the image of a Centaur cannot possibly be
produced from a single living creature, since an animal of   740
this type has never existed; but when the image of a
horse and that of a man happen to meet, they find it
easy to stick together at once, as we said before, due to
their rarefied nature and their flimsy texture. All other
things of this kind are made in the same way. As they

move nimbly with the utmost lightness, as I showed you   745
before, so it is that any single one of these superfine
images can stir the mind with a single blow, as the mind
itself is fine-textured and amazingly nimble.
You could easily recognise that these things happen in
the way I claim from the following; insofar as this which
we see with the mind looks like that which we see with   750
the eyes, it must be that they are produced in a like
manner.
Now since I have taught that I see a lion, say, by means
of images which stimulate the eyes, one may be sure that
the mind is stirred in a similar way by the images of lions   755
and all the other things it sees, stirred just as much and
no less than the eyes, except that the images it perceives
are finer in texture.
Nor is there any alternative explanation of why the
intellect of the mind is still awake when sleep has relaxed
the limbs, except that these same images still stimulate
our minds as they do when we are awake, and to such an   760
extent, that we seem to see quite clearly a man who has
left this life, a man whom death and earth have taken
captive. Nature forces this to happen thus because all the
sense organs of the body are blocked and dormant
throughout the limbs, and are unable to refute what is
false with reality. Besides, the memory lies dormant,   765
drooping in sleep, nor does it answer back that he, whom
the mind thinks it sees alive, has long since been in the
power of death and destruction.
Next, it is not surprising that images move, and fling
their arms and other limbs about in rhythm. For it does
happen that an image seems to do this in dreams; this is   770
because, when the first image perishes, the next one is
generated in a different position, and it looks as if the
first one has changed its stance. Of course this must be
imagined as a swift sequence: such is the agility, so
great is the quantity of things, so great is the quantity   775
of particles in any single moment of perception, to
maintain the supply. Many questions are raised in these
matters, many things need explaining, if we wish to set
out the subject clearly. The first question raised is this:
how is it that the mind can instantly think of whatever   780
we each desire (to see)? Do the images keep guard,
watching over our wishes, and does the image run up to
us as soon as we want it, whether it is sea, land or sky

quae cum mobiliter summa levitate feruntur,   745
ut prius ostendi, facile uno commovet ictu
quaelibet una animum nobis subtilis imago;
tenvis enim mens est et mire mobilis ipsa.
haec fieri ut memoro, facile hinc cognoscere possis.
quatenus hoc simile est illi, quod mente videmus   750
atque oculis, simili fieri ratione necesse est.
nunc igitur docui quoniam me forte leonem
cernere per simulacra, oculos quaecumque lacessunt,
scire licet mentem simili ratione moveri
per simulacra leonum et cetera quae videt aeque   755
nec minus atque oculi, nisi quod mage tenvia cernit.
nec ratione alia, cum somnus membra profudit,
mens animi vigilat, nisi quod simulacra lacessunt
haec eadem nostros animos quae cum vigilamus,
usque adeo, certe ut videamur cernere eum quem   760
rellicta vita iam mors et terra potitast.
hoc ideo fieri cogit natura, quod omnes
corporis offecti sensus per membra quiescunt
nec possunt falsum veris convincere rebus.
praeterea meminisse iacet languetque sopore,   765
nec dissentit eum mortis letique potitum
iam pridem, quem mens vivum se cernere credit.
quod superest, non est mirum simulacra moveri
bracchiaque in numerum iactare et cetera membra.
nam fit ut in somnis facere hoc videatur imago;   770
quippe·ubi prima perit alioque est altera nata
inde statu, prior hic gestum mutasse videtur.† 800-|
scilicet id fieri celeri ratione putandumst:
†tanta est mobilitas et rerum copia tanta, |- 799
tantaque sensibili quovis est tempore in uno   775
copia particularum, ut possit suppeditare.

multaque in his rebus quaeruntur multaque nobis
clarandumst, plane si res exponere avemus.
quaeritur in primis quare, quod cuique libido
venerit, extemplo mens cogitet eius id ipsum.   780
anne voluntatem nostram simulacra tuentur
et simul ac volumus nobis occurrit imago,
si mare, si terram cordist, si denique caelum?

---

755 leonum *OQ*: leonem *Lachmann*
761 rellicta *Voss*: reddita *OQ*

conventus hominum pompam convivia pugnas,
omnia sub verbone creat natura paratque?   785
cum praesertim aliis eadem in regione locoque
longe dissimilis animus res cogitet omnis.
quid porro, in numerum procedere cum simulacra
cernimus in somnis et mollia membra movere,
mollia mobiliter cum alternis bracchia mittunt   790
et repetunt oculis gestum pede convenienti?
 scilicet arte madent simulacra et docta vagantur,
nocturno facere ut possint in tempore ludos.
an magis illud erit verum? quia tempore in uno,
cum sentimus, id est, cum vox emittitur una,   795
tempora multa latent, ratio quae comperit esse,
propterea fit uti quovis in tempore quaeque
praesto sint simulacra locis in quisque parata:
⊣ tanta est mobilitas et rerum copia tanta.⊢ 774
hoc,⊣ubi prima perit alioque est altera nata   800
inde statu, prior hic gestum mutasse videtur.⊢ 771-2
et quia tenvia sunt, nisi quae contendit, acute
cernere non potis est animus; proinde omnia quae sunt
praeterea pereunt, nisi si ad quae se ipse paravit.
ipse parat sese porro speratque futurum   805
ut videat quod consequitur rem quamque; fit ergo.
nonne vides oculos etiam, cum tenvia quae sunt   (807)
cernere coeperunt, contendere se atque parare,   (809)
nec sine eo fieri posse ut cernamus acute?   (810)
et tamen in rebus quoque apertis noscere possis,
si non advertas animum, proinde esse quasi omni
tempore semotum fuerit longeque remotum.
cur igitur mirumst, animus si cetera perdit
praeterquam quibus est in rebus deditus ipse?   815
deinde adopinamur de signis maxima parvis
ac nos in fraudem induimus frustraminis ipsi.
fit quoque ut interdum non suppeditetur imago
eiusdem generis, sed femina quae fuit ante,
in manibus vir uti factus videatur adesse,   820
aut alia ex alia facies aetasque sequatur.
quod ne miremur sopor atque oblivia curant.   (826)

---

791 oculis *OQ*: ollis *Creech*
808 = 804 *omisit editio Aldina*
822 (826) *huc transtulit Q'*:

that we desire? Public assemblies, procession, banquets, battles – does nature fashion and prepare everything to 785 order? Especially since other people in the same locality and situation may have their minds thinking of all kinds of things that are nothing like each other. And what then of those times that we see images moving forward in dreams, stirring their supple limbs, nimbly flinging their supple arms alternately and repeating the position before 790 our eyes in a suitable rhythm?

The images must be soaked with skill, well-trained peripatetics, to be able to put on a show at night time. Or will this be closer to the truth? In one moment of perception, that is, in the time it takes for a single 795 sound to be uttered, there are many moments hidden which the intellect can grasp, and so at any one moment any images you like are ready to hand anywhere; such is their nimbleness, so great the supply of things. So, when 800 the first image perishes and the next one is generated in a different position, it looks as if the earlier one has changed its stance. Because they are flimsy, the mind can only discern the fine detail of those that it strains to see; besides, all the images perish, save those for which the mind has prepared itself. What is more, it prepares 805 itself and hopes that it will turn out that it can see that which immediately follows each thing – and so it does. Don't you see how the eyes strain and prepare themselves, when they are beginning to discern fine-textured things, and are incapable of discerning fine 810 detail unless they do so? And yet there are obvious cases in which you could recognise that if you fail to pay attention to something, it is as if it were completely removed in space and time. Why then is it strange if the mind loses all other images apart from the things it is 815 concentrating upon? Then we make massive assertions on the basis of minuscule evidence and shackle ourselves of our own accord in the deceit of delusion. It also happens sometimes that the image which is supplied is of a different kind; what used to be a woman seems to stand there now changed in our hands into a man, or 820 incongruous appearances and ages follow each other. Sleep and forgetfulness see to it that we feel no surprise at this.

illud in his rebus vitium vementer avemus
te fugere, errorem vitareque praemetuenter,
lumina ne facias oculorum clara creata,   825 (824)
prospicere ut possimus, et ut proferre queamus
proceros passus, ideo fastigia posse
surarum ac feminum pedibus fundata plicari,
bracchia tum porro validis ex apta lacertis
esse manusque datas utraque ex parte ministras,   830
ut facere ad vitam possemus quae foret usus.
cetera de genere hoc inter quaecumque pretantur,
omnia perversa praepostera sunt ratione,
nil ideo quoniam natumst in corpore ut uti
possemus, sed quod natumst id procreat usum.   835
nec fuit ante videre oculorum lumina nata,
nec dictis orare prius quam lingua creatast,
sed potius longe linguae praecessit origo
sermonem, multoque creatae sunt prius aures
quam sonus est auditus, et omnia denique membra   840
ante fuere, ut opinor, eorum quam foret usus;
haud igitur potuere utendi crescere causa.
at contra conferre manu certamina pugnae
et lacerare artus foedareque membra cruore
ante fuit multo quam lucida tela volarent,   845
et vulnus vitare prius natura coegit
quam daret obiectum parmai laeva per artem.
scilicet et fessum corpus mandare quieti
multo antiquius est quam lecti mollia strata,
et sedare sitim prius est quam pocula natum.   850
haec igitur possunt utendi cognita causa
credier, ex usu quae sunt vitaque reperta.
illa quidem seorsum sunt omnia quae prius ipsa
nata dedere suae post notitiam utilitatis.
quo genere in primis sensus et membra videmus;   855
quare etiam atque etiam procul est ut credere possis
utilitatis ob officium potuisse creari.
illud item non est mirandum, corporis ipsa
quod natura cibum quaerit cuiusque animantis.
quippe etenim fluere atque recedere corpora rebus   860
multa modis multis docui, sed plurima debent
ex animalibu'. quae quia sunt exercita motu
multaque per sudorem ex alto pressa feruntur,

---

823 avemus *Bernays*: inesse *OQ*
824 te fugere *Bailey*: effugere *OQ*

In this subject there is a particular fault that we
violently desire you to escape, a deviation to avoid with
caution; it is the opinion that the lights of the eyes were   825
created bright so that we could see our way, and that
the tops of our calves and thighs are based on feet and
also flexible just so that we should be able to stride
forward, and then that the lower arms are fastened to
sturdy upper arms and supplied with hands on each side   830
as servants, so that we could do whatever was needful to
stay alive. All other explanatory theories of this type are
also all back to front and logically upside down, since
nothing is created in the body for the purpose of us
being able to use it, but rather that which is generated   835
creates the use. There was no sight until the lights of
the eyes were born, no verbal pleading before the
creation of the tongue; on the contrary, the origin of the
tongue came long before speech, ears were created long
before sound was heard, in fact I believe all parts of the   840
body existed before there was a use for them;
thus they cannot have grown with the purpose of being
used. On the contrary, the hand-to-hand combat of
fighting, tearing of limbs and besmirching of parts of the
body with blood all happened long before the gleaming   845
weapons started to fly, nature forced men to avoid injury
before the left arm supplied the barrier of a shield by
the use of skill. Committing the tired body to rest is of
much greater antiquity than the soft coverlets of a bed,   850
quenching the thirst came about before drinking cups.
These things, which were discovered through experience
and life, can be thought to have been invented for their
purpose; but all those other things are quite distinct,
things which came into existence first and only afterwards
gave men the idea of their usefulness. In this class we   855
see especially the senses and the limbs; so I insist that it
would be far from the truth for you to believe that they
could have been created to fulfil the function of their
usefulness.
Similarly, there is no cause for surprise that it is the
nature of every living body to seek food, by instinct.
For I have taught you how particles flow and depart from   860
things in great numbers and in many ways – the greatest
number in fact come from living things, as they are kept
in motion, with many particles squeezed from deep down

57

multa per os exhalantur, cum languida anhelant,
his igitur rebus rarescit corpus et omnis   865
subruitur natura; dolor quam consequitur rem.
propterea capitur cibus, ut suffulciat artus
et recreet vires interdatus, atque patentem
per membra ac venas ut amorem obturet edendi.
umor item discedit in omnia quae loca cumque   870
poscunt umorem; glomerataque multa vaporis
corpora, quae stomacho praebent incendia nostro,
dissupat adveniens liquor ac restinguit ut ignem,
urere ne possit calor amplius aridus artus.
sic igitur tibi anhela sitis de corpore nostro   875
abluitur, sic expletur ieiuna cupido.

nunc qui fiat uti passus proferre queamus,
cum volumus, varieque datum sit membra movere,
et quae res tantum hoc oneris protrudere nostri
corporis insuerit, dicam; tu percipe dicta.   880
dico animo nostro primum simulacra meandi
accidere atque animum pulsare, ut diximus ante.
inde voluntas fit; neque enim facere incipit ullam
rem quisquam, quam mens providit quid velit ante;
id quod providet, illius rei constat imago.   885
ergo animus cum sese ita commovet ut velit ire
inque gredi, ferit extemplo quae in corpore toto
per membra atque artus animai dissita vis est;
et facilest factu, quoniam coniuncta tenetur.
inde ea proporro corpus ferit, atque ita tota   890
paulatim moles protruditur atque movetur.
praeterea tum rarescit quoque corpus, et aer
(scilicet ut debet qui semper mobilis extat)
per patefacta venit penetratque foramina largus,
et dispargitur ad partis ita quasque minutas   895
corporis. hic igitur rebus fit utrimque duabus,
corpus ut, ac navis velis ventoque, feratur.
nec tamen illud in his rebus mirabile constat,
tantula quod tantum corpus corpuscula possunt
contorquere et onus totum convertere nostrum.   900
quippe etenim ventus subtili corpore tenvis
trudit agens magnam magno molimine navem,
et manus una regit quantovis impete euntem
atque gubernaclum contorquet quolibet unum,
multaque per trocleas et tympana pondere magno   905

58

leaving in sweat, many exhaled through the mouth when
they pant with exhaustion; when this happens the body   865
loses density, its whole substance undermined. Pain
follows. For this reason food is taken to prop up the
limbs, to fill the gaps and restore our strength, to plug
the gaping desire to eat throughout the limbs and the
veins. In the same way fluid passes out into all those   870
parts that demand it, and as it arrives the liquid scatters
the multitudinous throng of heat particles which set fire
to our stomach, extinguishing them like a fire, to stop
the dry heat scorching our limbs. This, I tell you, is   875
how the panting thirst is washed away from our body,
this is how the famished longing is stuffed. Now I will
tell you how it comes about that we can move our steps
forward when we want, how we are endowed with a wide
range of limb movements, and what has got us into the
habit of shoving forward so great a load as this body of   880
ours; see that you grasp what I say. First of all, I tell
you, images of movement fall upon our mind and strike it,
as we said before. Then the desire forms – for nobody
ever begins to do anything until his mind has visualised
in advance what he wants, and his visualisation must be   885
made up of an image of that thing. Therefore when the
mind stirs itself so as to want to move and walk, it at
once strikes the power of the spirit which is scattered all
over the whole body throughout the bodily parts and the
limbs; nor is this difficult to do, as it is contained in
close connection with it.
Then the spirit strikes the body, and in this way the   890
whole mass is slowly shoved forward and moved. Also at
that time the pores widen in the body and air (as you
would expect in view of its permanent mobility) comes in
through the openings and works right into passages in
great quantities and so is spread out to every tiniest part   895
of the body. Here, then, thanks to two things acting in
two different ways, the body moves along like a ship with
both sails and wind. Nor, in discussing this, is there any
cause for surprise that such minute particles can impel so
large a body and shift our entire weight; for the wind is   900
flimsy with a rarefied substance, yet it drives and shoves
a massive ship with massive momentum; one single hand
controls it, however fast it is travelling, one rudder
diverts it in any direction; and a machine, using block
and tackle and revolving cylinders, moves many things of   905

commovet atque levi sustollit machina nisu.
nunc quibus ille modis somnus per membra quietem
inriget atque animi curas e pectore solvat,
suavidicis potius quam multis versibus edam;
parvus ut est cycni melior canor, ille gruum quam 910
clamor in aetheriis dispersus nubibus austri.   180-3
tu mihi da tenuis aures animumque sagacem,
ne fieri negites quae dicam posse, retroque
vera repulsanti discedas pectore dicta,
tutemet in culpa cum sis neque cernere possis.   915
principio somnus fit ubi est distracta per artus
vis animae partimque foras eiecta recessit
et partim contrusa magis concessit in altum;
dissoluuntur enim tum demum membra fluuntque.
nam dubium non est, animai quin opera sit   920
sensus hic in nobis, quem cum sopor inpedit esse,
tum nobis animam perturbatam esse putandumst
eiectamque foras; non omnem; namque iaceret
aeterno corpus perfusum frigore leti;
quippe ubi nulla latens animai pars remaneret   925
in membris, cinere ut multa latet obrutus ignis,
unde reconflari sensus per membra repente
posset, ut ex igni caeco consurgere flamma?
sed quibus haec rebus novitas confiat, et unde
perturbari anima et corpus languescere possit,   930
expediam; tu fac ne ventis verba profundam.
principio externa corpus de parte necessum est,
aeriis quoniam vicinum tangitur auris,
tundier atque eius crebro pulsarier ictu;
propptereaque fere res omnes aut corio sunt   935
aut etiam conchis aut callo aut cortice tectae.
interiorem etiam partem spirantibus aer
verberat hic idem, cum ducitur atque reflatur.
quare utrimque secus cum corpus vapulet, et cum
perveniant plagae per parva foramina nobis   940
corporis ad primas partis elementaque prima,
fit quasi paulatim nobis per membra ruina;
conturbantur enim positurae principiorum
corporis atque animi. fit uti pars inde animai
eiiciatur, et introrsum pars abdita cedat,   945

---

945 eiiciatur *Lambinus*: eliciatur *OQ*

60

great weight and raises them up with only a gentle push.
Now I shall explain how this sleep flushes rest through
the limbs and looses mental cares from the breast – I
shall explain this in verses that are more mellifluous than
numerous; just as the brief song of the swan is   910
preferable to that noise of cranes broadcast among the
southern clouds in the sky. Pay attention with keen ears
and a sharp mind to prevent you denying the possibility
of what I say, in case you go away with your heart
utterly rejecting my words of truth when it is you   915
yourself who are to blame and are unable to discern the
truth. Firstly, sleep occurs when the force of the spirit
is pulled to pieces throughout the limbs, some of it being
expelled and leaving altogether and some of it being
packed in closer compression and retreating into the
depths – not until then do the limbs lose their tension   920
and become fluid. For there is no doubt that this
sensation of ours is the work of the spirit, and at those
times when sleep interferes with our consciousness we
must conclude that the spirit is thrown into confusion and
driven out of the body: not all of it, however, or else
our body would be lying soaked in the eternal chill of   925
death. For if no part of the spirit remained latent in the
limbs, like a fire hidden and buried in a heap of ashes,
from what source could sensation be suddenly fanned into
flame again throughout the limbs, as flame can spring up
from unseen fire? I will explain by what means this new
state of affairs comes about, and the source of the   930
disturbance of the soul and the relaxation of the body:
you see to it that I do not pour out my words to the
winds.
First of all it must be that since the outside surface of
the body borders on the breezes of the air and is
touched by them it is thumped and beaten by the
constant impact; for this reason virtually everything is   935
covered either with skin or shells or rind or bark. This
same air flogs the inside part of the body in respiration
as it is brought in and then blown back again. Therefore
since the body is thrashed both ways separately, and
since the blows pierce right through to the primary parts   940
and the most basic elements of the body, passing through
tiny channels, there thus occurs something akin to a
gradual demolition throughout the limbs, for the relative
positions of mind atoms and body atoms are mixed up.
The consequence is that part of the spirit is expelled,   945

61

pars etiam distracta per artus non queat esse
coniuncta inter se neque motu mutua fungi;
inter enim saepit coetus natura viasque;
ergo sensus abit mutatis motibus alte.
et quoniam non est quasi quod suffulciat artus,   950
debile fit corpus languescuntque omnia membra,
bracchia palpebraeque cadunt poplitesque cubanti
saepe tamen summittuntur virisque resolvunt.
deinde cibum sequitur somnus, quia, quae facit aer,
haec eadem cibus, in venas dum diditur omnis,   955
efficit. et multo sopor ille gravissimus exstat
quem satur aut lassus capias, quia plurima tum se
corpora conturbant magno contusa labore.
fit ratione eadem coniectus partim animai
altior atque foras eiectus largior eius,   960
et divisior inter se ac distractior intus.
et quo quisque fere studio devinctus adhaeret,
aut quibus in rebus multum sumus ante morati,
atque in ea ratione fuit contenta magis mens,
in somnis eadem plerumque videmur obire: 965
causidici causas agere et componere leges,
induperatores pugnare ac proelia obire,
nautae contractum cum ventis degere duellum,
nos agere hoc autem et naturam quaerere rerum
semper et inventam patriis exponere chartis.   970
cetera sic studia atque artes plerumque videntur
in somnis animos hominum frustrata tenere.
et quicumque dies multos ex ordine ludis
adsiduas dederunt operas, plerumque videmus,
cum iam destiterunt ea sensibus usurpare,   975
relicuas tamen esse vias in mente patentis,
qua possint eadem rerum simulacra venire.
per multos itaque illa dies eadem obversantur
ante oculos, etiam vigilantes ut videantur
cernere saltantis et mollia membra moventis,   980
et citharae liquidum carmen chordasque loquentis
auribus accipere, et consessum cernere eundem
scenaique simul varios splendere decores.

---

959 partim *Lachmann*: parte *OQ*
961 intus *OQ*: actus *Lachmann*: intust *W. Everett*
968 duellum *cod. Bodleianus*: vellum *O*: velum *Q*: bellum
O corr.

part passes inwards in hiding, and another part is torn
apart throughout the limbs, losing its internal cohesion
and its ability to perform an interacting movement; this is
because nature barricades the confluences and pathways,
and the deep change in movements produces the loss of
sensation. Since there is nothing which could, as it were,   950
prop up the limbs, the body becomes weak, the limbs
grow slack, arms and eyelids droop, legs often buckle
underneath you as you lie down and relax their strength.
Then too sleep follows food because food acts like air
when it is despatched out to all the veins, with the same   955
effect. Much the deepest sleep is that which you take
when replete or tired, because the maximum number of
atoms are mixed up at that time, deadened with great
effort. In the same way the partial thrusting down of the
spirit is deeper, the expulsion out of the body is more   960
generous and the internal division and dispersal is
greater. Whatever enthusiasm each of us is attached and
addicted to, or whatever things we have spent a good
deal of time on in the past, our mind more captivated with
that (than anything else), it is generally these same   965
things that we seem to encounter in dreams; barristers
think they are pleading cases and matching law against
law, generals fighting and joining battles, sailors
undertaking and waging a war with the winds; I dream
that I am doing this, constantly seeking the nature of
things and when I find it setting it out in my native   970
language. All other enthusiasms and skills also seem
generally to grip men's minds in this way in dreams,
deluding them. If anyone has given his whole attention
constantly to the games for many days in succession, we
generally see that, although he has stopped receiving   975
these (images) through the senses, channels remain open
in his mind by which these same images of things may
come to him. So for many days the same images move
before his eyes, so that even when he is awake he seems   980
to see dancers stirring their supple limbs, to perceive in
his ears the fluent song of the lyre and its speaking
strings, to see the same audience and the different
beauties of the stage shine brilliantly. This is how

63

usque adeo magni refert studium atque voluptas,
et quibus in rebus consuerint esse operati   985
non homines solum, sed vero animalia cuncta.
quippe videbis equos fortis, cum membra iacebunt,
in somnis sudare tamen spirareque semper
et quasi de palma summas contendere viris,
aut quasi carceribus patefactis fundere sese.   990
venantumque canes in molli saepe quiete   (999)
iactant crura tamen subito vocesque repente   (991)
mittunt et crebro redducunt naribus auras
ut vestigia si teneant inventa ferarum,
expergefactique sequuntur inania saepe   995   (994
cervorum simulacra, fugae quasi dedita cernant,
donec discussis redeant erroribus ad se.
at consueta domi catulorum blanda propago
discutere et corpus de terra corripere instant   999   (998
proinde quasi ignotas facies atque ora tuantur.   1004
et quo quaeque magis sunt aspera seminiorum,   1005
tam magis in somnis eadem saevire necessust.
at variae fugiunt volucres pinnisque repente
sollicitant divum nocturno tempore lucos,
accipitres somno in leni si proelia pugnas
edere sunt persectantes visaeque volantes.   1010
porro hominum mentes, magnis quae motibus edunt
magna, itidem saepe in somnis faciuntque geruntque
reges expugnant, capiuntur, proelia miscent,
tollunt clamorem, quasi si iugulentur ibidem.
multi depugnant gemitusque doloribus edunt   1015
et, quasi pantherae morsu saevive leonis
mandantur, magnis clamoribus omnia complent.
multi de magnis per somnum rebu' loquuntur
indicioque sui facti persaepe fuere.
multi mortem obeunt. multi, de montibus altis   1020
ut qui praecipitent ad terram corpore toto,
exterruntur, et ex somno quasi mentibu' capti
vix ad se redeunt, permoti corporis aestu.
flumen item sitiens aut fontem propter amoenum

---

984 voluptas *Lachmann*: voluntas *OQ*
990 fundere sese *Richter*: rumpere sese *M. F. Smith*:
saepe quiete *OQ: alii alia*
991 (999) *huc transtulit ed. Aldina*
1000-3 = 992-5
1022 exterruntur *OQ*: exterrentur *ed. Aldina*

important enthusiasm and pleasure are, as well as the 985
habitual activities which not only humans but in fact all
living creatures practise. So you will see sturdy horses,
when their limbs are lying flat, still sweating in sleep,
panting constantly, as if they were straining themselves
to the limit to win the palm, or racing off out of the 990
stalls as they open. Hunters' dogs in cosy sleep often
toss their legs suddenly, utter unexpected barks and
keep sniffing the air in their nostrils, as if they had
found the tracks of wild beasts and were clinging on to
them. When awoken they often chase after the empty 995
images of stags, as if they saw them intent on flight,
until they shake off their illusions and return to
themselves. The fawning breed of domestic dogs rush to 999
shake themselves and to whip their bodies from off the
ground exactly as if they saw strange faces and forms. 1005
The rougher the breed, the more savage their dreams
must be. The various types of birds fly away, suddenly
startling the groves of the gods at night time with their
wings, if they dream in their quiet sleep that hawks are 1010
flying in pursuit of them to offer battles and fights.
Furthermore the minds of men, which bring forth great
deeds with great movements, often behave and perform in
the same way in sleep: kings sack cities, are captured,
engage in battles, raise a shout as if their throats were
being slit then and there. Many fight in the arena, 1015
groaning with pain, filling the whole place with great
screams as if they were being chewed up by the jaws of a
panther or a savage lion. Many people talk of important
matters in sleep and have very often laid evidence against
their own deed. Many die. Many are terrified, as if they 1020
were falling head over heels to the earth from high
mountains, and when they wake they are like madmen,
finding it hard to return to their senses, disturbed by
the confusion of their body. The thirsty man sits next to
a river or a pleasant spring and takes in virtually the 1025

adsidet et totum prope faucibus occupat amnem.   1025
parvi saepe lacum propter si ac dolia curta
somno devincti credunt se extollere vestem,
totius umorem saccatum corpori' fundunt,
cum Babylonica magnifico splendore rigantur.
tum quibus aetatis freta primitus insinuatur   1030
semen, ubi ipsa dies membris matura creavit,
conveniunt simulacra foris e corpore quoque,
nuntia praeclari voltus pulchrique coloris,
qui ciet inritans loca turgida semine multo,
ut quasi transactis saepe omnibu' rebu' profundant   1035
fluminis ingentis fluctus vestemque cruentent.

sollicitatur id in nobis, quod diximus ante,
semen, adulta aetas cum primum roborat artus.
namque alias aliud res commovet atque lacessit;
ex homine humanum semen ciet una hominis vis.   1040
quod simul atque suis eiectum sedibus exit,
per membra atque artus decedit corpore toto
in loca conveniens nervorum certa, cietque
continuo partis genitalis corporis ipsas.
inritata tument loca semine, fitque voluntas   1045
eicere id quo se contendit dira libido,   (1046)
idque petit corpus, mens unde est saucia amore;   (1048)
namque omnes plerumque cadunt in vulnus, et illam
emicat in partem sanguis unde icimur ictu,   1050
et si comminus est, hostem ruber occupat umor.
sic igitur Veneris qui telis accipit ictus,
sive puer membris muliebribus hunc iaculatur
seu mulier toto iactans e corpore amorem,
unde feritur, eo tendit gestitque coire   1055
et iacere umorem in corpus de corpore ductum;
namque voluptatem praesagit muta cupido.
haec Venus est nobis; hinc autemst nomen amoris;
hinc illaec primum Veneris dulcedinis in cor
stillavit gutta, et successit frigida cura.   1060
nam si abest quod ames, praesto simulacra tamen sunt
illius, et nomen dulce obversatur ad auris.
sed fugitare decet simulacra et pabula amoris

1026 parvi *M.L. Clarke*: puri *OQ*: multi *Avancius*: poti
Merrill
1047 = 1034 *excl. Naugerius*

whole stream in his jaws. Often children think they are
lifting up their clothes next to a urinal or low storage jar
when they are bound in sleep and gush forth the filtered
liquid of their whole body, and the Babylonian coverlets
in their opulent brilliance are soaked through.
Then boys in whom the seed is for the first time working 1030
its way into the rough seas of their youth, when time
itself in its maturity has created the seed in their limbs,
these boys are encountered by images from outside,
images from any and every body, images heralding a
gorgeous face and a beautiful complexion which awakes
and stimulates the parts, swollen with excess seed, so 1035
that just as if the whole job had been done they often
spurt out the flood of a massive river and stain their
clothes.
This seed is aroused in us, as we said earlier, when the
age of maturity first stiffens our limbs. For different
stimuli excite and provoke different things; but only the
power of a human being can awake the human seed from a 1040
human body. As soon as it is evicted from its abodes it
makes its way out, passing through the limbs and the
joints all over the body, gathering at the specific region
of the groin and at once awakening the actual genital
parts of the body. These parts are stimulated and swell 1045
with seed, and there then comes the urge to eject it in
the direction in which the awful lust is pulling, the body
making for that which has wounded the mind with love;
for everybody usually falls in the direction of a wound, 1050
the blood gushes out towards the place from where we
received the blow which hit us, and, if the fighting is at
close quarters, the red fluid soaks our enemy. Thus,
then, anyone who sustains the blows of Venus – whether
the source of the blow is a boy with womanish limbs
shooting him, or a woman sending out love from her whole
body – he lunges towards the source of the blow, 1055
struggling to unite and to ejaculate the fluid drawn from
his body into that body; for his dumb lust foretells
pleasure.
This is Venus to us; this is where love derives its name;
this is where that drop of Venus' sweetness came from
which first dripped into our heart, to be succeeded by 1060
icy anxiety. For if the object of your love is not there,
the images are still to hand and the sweet name rings in
the ears. The right thing to do is to run away from the

67

absterrere sibi atque alio convertere mentem
et iacere umorem conlectum in corpora quaeque,   1065
nec retinere, semel conversum unius amore,
et servare sibi curam certumque dolorem;
ulcus enim vivescit et inveterascit alendo,
inque dies gliscit furor atque aerumna gravescit,
si non prima novis conturbes vulnera plagis   1070
vulgivagaque vagus Venere ante recentia cures
aut alio possis animi traducere motus.
nec Veneris fructu caret is qui vitat amorem,
sed potius quae sunt sine poena commoda sumit;
nam certe purast sanis magis inde voluptas   1075
quam miseris. etenim potiundi tempore in ipso
fluctuat incertis erroribus ardor amantum,
nec constat quid primum oculis manibusque fruantur.
quod petiere, premunt arte faciuntque dolorem
corporis, et dentes inlidunt saepe labellis   1080
osculaque adfligunt, quia non est pura voluptas
et stimuli subsunt qui instigant laedere id ipsum,
quodcumque est, rabies unde illaec germina surgunt.
sed leviter poenas frangit Venus inter amorem,
blandaque refrenat morsus admixta voluptas;   1085
namque in eo spes est, unde est ardoris origo,
restingui quoque posse ab eodem corpore flammam.
quod fieri contra totum natura repugnat:
unaque res haec est, cuius quam plurima habemus,
tam magis ardescit dira cuppedine pertus.   1090
nam cibus atque umor membris adsumitur intus;
quae quoniam certas possunt obsidere partis,
hoc facile expletur laticum frugumque cupido.
ex hominis vero facie pulchroque colore
nil datur in corpus praeter simulacra fruendum   1095
tenvia; quae vento spes raptast saepe misella.
ut bibere in somnis sitiens cum quaerit et umor
non datur, ardorem qui membris stinguere possit,
sed laticum simulacra petit frustraque laborat
in medioque sitit torrenti flumine potans,   1100
sic in amore Venus simulacris ludit amantis,

1096 raptast *Munro*: raptat *OQ*

images, to scare off those things that feed love, to direct
the mind elsewhere, to ejaculate the build-up of fluid into 1065
bodies indiscriminately rather than hold on to it, obsessed
with the love of one person only and thus saving up
love-sickness and inevitable pain for oneself; for the sore
quickens and turns chronic if it is nourished, the
madness gets worse day by day, the trouble becomes
more depressing if you do not confound the original 1070
wounds with new blows, treating them in time while they
are still fresh by roaming about in sexual promiscuity or
else transferring the movements of the mind in another
direction. Nor does the man who avoids love go without
the enjoyment of sex - on the contrary, he takes the
rewards without paying the penalty; there is no doubt 1075
that the pleasure is less contaminated for the sane than it
is for pining lovers. For even in the moment of
possession the burning passion of lovers is storm-tossed
in indecisive wandering off course with no fixed target
for them to enjoy first with eyes and hands. They
squeeze the object of their desire tightly and cause 1080
physical pain, they often bite right into the lips in a
violent collision of kisses because their pleasure is
contaminated and instincts lurk to goad them unto hurting
that very thing - whatever it is - from which those buds
of madness grow.
But in the middle of their love Venus gives them a gentle
break in the punishment, and affectionate pleasure is 1085
mingled in and reins in the bites; for therein lies the
hope that the flame can be extinguished by the same body
which gave rise to the burning passion. Nature however
stops this from ever happening; this is the only thing of
which, however much we have, the breast only burns 1090
with ever more awful lust. For food and liquid are
absorbed in the limbs, and as the parts which they can
occupy are limited, the desire for water and bread is
easily filled. But nothing comes from the looks of a human 1095
being and a pretty complexion which can pass into the
body, to be enjoyed, except insubstantial images, and so
the love-sick hope is often whipped off in the wind. Just
as when a thirsty man is trying to drink and water is not
given him to put out the flames of desire in his limbs; he
makes for the images of water, toiling in vain, in the 1100
middle of a rushing river he is thirsty as he drinks; this
is how it is in the case of love when Venus teases lovers

nec satiare queunt spectando corpora coram,
nec manibus quicquam teneris abradere membris
possunt errantes incerti corpore toto.
denique cum membris conlatis flore fruuntur   1105
aetatis, iam cum praesagit gaudia corpus
atque in eost Venus ut muliebria conserat arva,
adfigunt avide corpus iunguntque salivas
oris et inspirant pressantes dentibus ora,
nequiquam, quoniam nil inde abradere possunt   1110
nec penetrare et abire in corpus corpore toto;
nam facere interdum velle et certare videntur:
usque adeo cupide in Veneris compagibus haerent,
membra voluptatis dum vi labefacta liquescunt.
tandem ubi se erupit nervis conlecta cupido,   1115
parva fit ardoris violenti pausa parumper.
inde redit rabies eadem et furor ille revisit,
cum sibi quod cupiant ipsi contingere quaerunt,
nec reperire malum id possunt quae machina vincat:
usque adeo incerti tabescunt vulnere caeco.   1120

adde quod absumunt viris pereuntque labore,
adde quod alterius sub nutu degitur aetas.
labitur interea res et Babylonica fiunt,
languent officia atque aegrotat fama vacillans.
unguenta et pulchra in pedibus Sicyonia rident;   1125
scilicet et grandes viridi cum luce zmaragdi
auro includuntur, teriturque thalassina vestis
adsidue et Veneris sudorem exercita potat;
et bene parta patrum fiunt anademata, mitrae,
interdum in pallam ac Melitensia Coaque vertunt;   1130
eximia veste et victu convivia, ludi,
pocula crebra, unguenta, coronae, serta parantur;
nequiquam, quoniam medio de fonte leporum
surgit amari aliquid quod in ipsis floribus angat,
aut cum conscius ipse animus se forte remordet   1135
desidiose agere aetatem lustrisque perire,
aut quod in ambiguo verbum iaculata reliquit

1118 quod cupiant *OQ*: quod cupiunt *A*: quid cupiant
Lachmann
1125 unguenta *OQ*: argentum *Lachmann*: ingenue *A*. *Allen*
1130 ac Melitensia *Lambinus*: atque Alidensia *OQ*: Coaque
Bergk: Chiaque *OQ*

with images, and merely looking at bodies cannot satisfy them, even if they are face to face; neither can they remove any part from the delicate limbs by rubbing them with their hands as they wander at random all over the body. Then, when they have joined their limbs together 1105 and are enjoying the flower of youth, when the body senses the joys to come and Venus is on the point of sowing the female fields, they hug their body greedily, they mingle together the saliva of their mouth, they breathe hard down each other's mouths, pressing them with their teeth. It is all a waste of effort, as they 1110 cannot remove any bit of it by rubbing, nor can they get right inside that body and make their whole body disappear in it – for sometimes this is what they seem to want and to strive for. So lustfully are they stuck in the bonds of Venus, while their limbs totter and turn to water with the force of the pleasure. When at last the built-up lust has burst out of their groin, there is then a 1115 short respite from the burning passion, just for a little while. Then the same frenzy, the old madness comes back again when they seek to obtain a suitable object for their lust and cannot find any mechanical means of overcoming this trouble – to such an extent do they rot away 1120 aimlessly with their secret sore.

Note also that they wear out their strength and work themselves to death; note also that their life is passed under the capricious control of somebody else. Their property slips away from them to become Babylonian coverlets, their responsibilities droop, their good name totters and falls sick. Perfumes and lovely slippers from 1125 Sicyon laugh on her feet, and of course massive emeralds with their green gleam are encased in gold, the sea-dyed garment is worn thin with constant use and drinks the sweat of Venus in the course of the exertions; the hard-earned legacy of fathers turns to hairbands, head-dresses, a cloak sometimes and garments from Malta 1130 and Cos; banquets are set up with exquisite decor and cuisine, games, plenty of drink, perfumes, garlands, festoons, but it is all a waste of time, since from the heart of the source of these delights there rises up a touch of bitterness which rankles even amid the flowers – perhaps when his guilty conscience pricks him with the 1135 thought that he is spending his life wantonly, ruining himself in sordid brothels; or because in leaving she has

71

quod cupido adfixum cordi vivescit ut ignis,
aut nimium iactare oculos aliumve tueri
quod putat, in vultuque videt vestigia risus.   1140
atque in amore mala haec proprio summeque secundo
inveniuntur; in adverso vero atque inopi sunt,
prendere quae possis oculorum lumine operto,
innumerabilia; ut melius vigilare sit ante,
qua docui ratione, cavereque ne inliciaris.   1145
nam vitare, plagas in amoris ne laciamur,
non ita difficile est quam captum retibus ipsis
exire et validos Veneris perrumpere nodos.
et tamen implicitus quoque possis inque peditus
effugere infestum, nisi tute tibi obvius obstes   1150
et praetermittas animi vitia omnia primum
aut quae corpori' sunt eius, quam praepetis ac vis.
nam faciunt homines plerumque cupidine caeci
et tribuunt ea quae non sunt his commoda vere.
multimodis igitur pravas turpisque videmus   1155
esse in deliciis summoque in honore vigere.
atque alios alii inrident Veneremque suadent
ut placent, quoniam foedo adflictentur amore,
nec sua respiciunt miseri mala maxima saepe.
nigra melichrus est, inmunda et fetida acosmos,   1160
caesia Palladium, nervosa et lignea dorcas,
parvula pumilio, chariton mia, tota merum sal,
magna atque inmanis cataplexis plenaque honoris.
balba loqui non quit, traulizi; muta, pudens est;
at flagrans odiosa loquacula Lampadium fit;   1165
ischnon eromenion tum fit cum vivere non quit
prae macie; rhadine verost iam mortua tussi;
at tumida et mammosa Ceres est, ipsa ab Iaccho;
simula Silena ac saturast, labeosa philema.
cetera de genere hoc longum est si dicere coner.   1170
sed tamen esto iam quantovis oris honore,
cui Veneris membris vis omnibus exoriatur:
nempe aliae quoque sunt; nempe hac sine viximus ante;

1146 laciamur *Lambinus* : iaciamur *OQ*

shot an equivocal word at him which lodges in his pining
heart and kindles like fire; or because he thinks she is
casting her glances too freely or gazing at another man,
and he sees the traces of a laugh on her face.   1140
These are the troubles that are found in a love which is
proper and supremely successful; but in unsuccessful,
unrequited love there are countless troubles that you
could grasp even with your eyes shut – which is why it
is better to watch out before it happens, in the way I   1145
have taught you, and to beware of being enticed. For it
is not so hard to avoid being inveigled into the snares of
love as it is to escape from the nets themselves once you
are caught and to break your way through the powerful
knots of Venus. Yet even when you are entangled and
encumbered you could still escape the danger if you do not 1150
stand in your own way and start ignoring all the mental
and physical defects of her whom you are pursuing and
desiring above all others.
For this is what men usually do when blinded with lust,
claiming that women have assets which are simply not
there. This is how we see women who are in many ways   1155
foul and disgusting regarded as sweethearts, thriving in
the highest esteem. Lovers mock each other, urging each
other to appease Venus as they are smitten with a
disgraceful infatuation, failing to notice their own colossal
problems in their love-sick pathetic state. The swarthy 1160
girl is 'honey-coloured', a filthy stinking slut is 'beauty
unadorned', the green-eyed one is 'the image of Pallas';
if she is stringy, as soft as a plank of wood, she's a
'gazelle'; a stunted pygmy is 'one of the Graces', 'pure
sparkle all over'; the massive dragon is 'knock-out', 'a
fine figure of a woman'; she can't speak for stammering –
'she lisps'; the dumb girl is 'shy'; the blazing hateful 1165
gossip is a 'livewire'; she's 'slender', 'a little love' when
she's nearly dead from emaciation; she's 'svelte' when
she's all but coughed herself to death; the fat girl with
enormous breasts is 'Ceres herself, feeding Iacchus'; the
girl with the stumpy little nose is a 'faun', a 'lady
Satyr'; the one with balloon lips is 'all one big kiss'. To
try to mention all the other euphemisms of this kind would 1170
be a time-consuming business. Yet all the same, however
respectable her face, even if the power of Venus streams
out of her every limb, there are still other women as
well; we managed to live without her before; she does

73

nempe eadem facit, et scimus facere, omnia turpi,
et miseram taetris se suffit odoribus ipsa,   1175
quam famulae longe fugitant furtimque cachinnant.
at lacrimans exclusus amator limina saepe
floribus et sertis operit postisque superbos
unguit amaracino et foribus miser oscula figit;
quem si, iam ammissum, venientem offenderit aura   1180
una modo, causas abeundi quaerat honestas,
et meditata diu cadat alte sumpta querella,
stultitiaque ibi se damnet, tribuisse quod illi
plus videat quam mortali concedere par est.
nec Veneres nostras hoc fallit; quo magis ipsae   1185
omnia summo opere hos vitae postscaenia celant
quos retinere volunt adstrictosque esse in amore;
nequiquam, quoniam tu animo tamen omnia possis
protrahere in lucem atque omnis inquirere risus,
et, si bello animost et non odiosa, vicissim   1190
praetermittere et humanis concedere rebus.
nec mulier semper ficto suspirat amore
quae conplexa viri corpus cum corpore iungit
et tenet adsuctis umectans oscula labris;
nam facit ex animo saepe et, communia quaerens   1195
gaudia, sollicitat spatium decurrere amoris.
nec ratione alia volucres armenta feraeque
et pecudes et equae maribus subsidere possent,
si non ipsa quoque illarum subat ardet abundans
natura et Venerem salientum laeta retractat.   1200
nonne vides etiam quos mutua saepe voluptas
vinxit, ut in vinclis communibus excrucientur?
in triviis cum saepe canes, discedere aventes,
diversi cupide summis ex viribu' tendunt,
cum interea validis Veneris compagibus haerent.   1205 (1210)
quod facerent numquam, nisi mutua gaudia nossent   (1204)
quae lacere in fraudem possent vinctosque tenere.
quare etiam atque etiam, ut dico, est communi' voluptas.

et commiscendo cum semine forte virilem
femina vim vicit subita vi corripuitque,   1210 (1209)
tum similes matrum materno semine fiunt,

1198 possent *OQ*: possunt *Lachmann*
1199 quoque *Brieger*: quod *OQ*
1207 lacere *Lambinus*: iacere *OQ*

just the same things – and we know she does – as the
slut, fumigating her pathetic body with her disgusting 1175
smells, causing the maids to run a mile and snigger at
her behind her back.
But the tearful locked-out lover keeps covering the
threshold with flowers and garlands, anointing the proud
door-posts with marjoram and planting kisses pathetically 1180
on the door. Yet suppose she let him in – just one single
sniff of the air on his way in and he'd be looking for
decent excuses to clear off, his long-planned elegy,
drawn from the bottom of his heart, would fall to bits;
then he'd curse himself for being stupid enough to credit
her with qualities more than mortal. Our own goddesses 1185
of love are well aware of this; that is why they do all in
their power to keep all the back-stage realities of life
from those men whom they want to keep fettered in the
bonds of love. It's no use. Just by thinking about it you
could drag them all out to expose them to the light and
find out what is behind all the giggling. Then, if the 1190
woman is kind-hearted and not given to spite, you could
in turn decide to turn a blind eye and make allowances
for what is only human.
Nor does a woman always fake her love when she sighs,
joining her body with her man's body in an embrace,
clinging to his kisses with the wet suction of her lips;
often she is acting quite sincerely, longing for mutual 1195
joys, when she stimulates him to run the race of love
right to the finish. How else could birds, cattle, beasts
and mares stay under the males, unless their own nature
were also overflowing, on heat, burning with passion,
thrusting with delight against the penis of the leaping 1200
males?
Don't you see how mutual pleasure has often bound them
together so much that they are tortured in their shared
bonds? Dogs at crossroads, yearning to separate, often
pull desperately with all their strength in different
directions, while all the time they are stuck together in 1205
the strong cementation of Venus. They would never do
this, if they had no notion of the shared joys which could
entice them into the trap and hold them fettered. All this
goes to show that, as I say, the pleasure is mutual. In
the mingling of the seed, at those times when the woman
has chanced to overpower the power of the man with a 1210
sudden show of power and seized the upper hand, then

ut patribus patrio. sed quos utriusque figurae
esse vides, iuxtim miscentes vulta parentum,
corpore de patrio et materno sanguine crescunt,
semina cum Veneris stimulis excita per artus   1215
obvia conflixit conspirans mutuus ardor,
et neque utrum superavit eorum nec superatumst.
fit quoque ut interdum similes existere avorum
possint et referant proavorum saepe figuras,
propterea quia multa modis primordia multis   1220
mixta suo celant in corpore saepe parentes,
quae patribus patres tradunt a stirpe profecta;
inde Venus varia producit sorte figuras
maiorumque refert vultus vocesque comasque
quandoquidem nilo minus haec de semine certo   1225
fiunt quam facies et corpora membraque nobis.
et muliebre oritur patrio de semine saeclum,
maternoque mares existunt corpore creti;
semper enim partus duplici de semine constat,
atque utri similest magis id quodcumque creatur,   1230
eius habet plus parte aequa; quod cernere possis,
sive virum suboles sivest muliebris origo.

nec divina satum genitalem numina cuiquam
absterrent, pater a gnatis ne dulcibus umquam
appelletur et ut sterili Venere exigat aevum;   1235
quod plerumque putant, et multo sanguine maesti
conspergunt aras adolentque altaria donis,
ut gravidas reddant uxores semine largo.
nequiquam divum numen sortisque fatigant;
nam steriles nimium crasso sunt semine partim,   1240
et liquido praeter iustum tenuique vicissim.
tenve locis quia non potis est adfigere adhaesum,
liquitur extemplo et revocatum cedit abortu.
crassius his porro quoniam concretius aequo
mittitur, aut non tam prolixo provolat ictu   1245
aut penetrare locos aeque nequit aut penetratum
aegre admiscetur muliebri semine semen.

1225 minus *Lambinus*: magis *OQ*

children are produced from the mother's seed which resemble the mother, just as those from the fathers' seed resemble the fathers. Those children that you see with the distinct characteristics of both, merging together their parents' faces, these children grow from the body of the father and the blood of the mother, when the seeds, awoken throughout the limbs by the goads of 1215 Venus, are forced into a head-on collision by the mutual passion in perfect concord, and neither of them has conquered or been conquered. It sometimes happens also that children are born looking like their grandfathers, and they often reproduce the features of great-grandfathers, because the parents often conceal 1220 many elements mixed together in many different ways in their body, which fathers hand down to fathers from the root of the race; in a lottery of endless possibilities Venus draws out features and reproduces the faces, voices and hair of their ancestors, which all arise from a 1225 specific seed no less than our appearance, bodies and limbs. And female offspring arise from the father's seed, and males come into existence grown from the mother's body because the birth always consists of the double seed, and the child that is produced has more than an 1230 equal share of that parent whom it resembles more than the other, as you could see whether it is the scion of men or a female birth.

Nor is it divine powers which frighten off the sowing of reproductive seed from anyone, preventing him from ever being called father by delightful children, forcing him to 1235 live out his life in unfruitful intercourse; yet most people think it is the gods, miserably spattering altars with great quantities of blood and setting them on fire with offerings, praying that they might render their wives heavy with vast amounts of seed. It is a waste of time for them to exhaust the power of the gods and the sacred lots; for they are sterile – some because their seed is too 1240 thick, then again in turn if their seed is inordinately watery and thin; thin, because it cannot cling and stick to the parts, and so runs down at once and retreats withdrawn in miscarriage. Seed that is too thick, because it is too solid when ejaculated, either cannot fly forward 1245 with so far-flung an impact, or cannot penetrate the parts so well, or if it does penetrate it finds it hard to mingle its seed with the seed of the woman.

nam multum harmoniae Veneris differre videntur.
atque alias alii complent magis, ex aliisque
succipiunt aliae pondus magis inque gravescunt.   1250
et multae steriles Hymenaeis ante fuerunt
pluribus, et nactae post sunt tamen unde puellos
suscipere et partu possent ditescere dulci.
et quibus ante domi fecundae saepe nequissent
uxores parere, inventast illis quoque compar   1255
natura, ut possent gnatis munire senectam.
usque adeo magni refert, ut semina possint
seminibus commisceri genitaliter apta,
crassaque conveniant liquidis et liquida crassis.
atque in eo refert quo victu vita colatur;   1260
namque aliis rebus concrescunt semina membris
atque aliis extenvantur tabentque vicissim.
et quibus ipsa modis tractetur blanda voluptas,
id quoque permagni refert; nam more ferarum
quadrupedumque magis ritu plerumque putantur   1265
concipere uxores, quia sic loca sumere possunt,
pectoribus positis, sublatis semina lumbis.
nec molles opu' sunt motus uxoribus hilum;
nam mulier prohibet se concipere atque repugnat,
clunibus ipsa viri Venerem si laeta retractat   1270
atque exossato ciet omni corpore fluctus;
eicit enim sulcum recta regione viaque
vomeris atque locis avertit seminis ictum.
idque sua causa consuerunt scorta moveri,
ne complerentur crebro gravidaeque iacerent,   1275
et simul ipsa viris Venus ut concinnior esset;
coniugibus quod nil nostris opus esse videtur.

nec divinitus interdum Venerisque sagittis
deteriore fit ut forma muliercula ametur;
nam facit ipsa suis interdum femina factis   1280
morigerisque modis et munde corpore culto,
ut facile insuescat te secum degere vitam.
quod superest, consuetudo concinnat amorem;
nam leviter quamvis quod crebro tunditur ictu,
vincitur in longo spatio tamen atque labascit.   1285

1271 corpore W. Clausen: pectore OQ
1282 te Bernays: om. OQ

For the ensembles of Venus seem to vary enormously.
Some men fill up some women more than others, some
women take up the burden and grow pregnant from some 1250
men more than others. Many women have been barren in a
succession of previous marriages, only to acquire mates
later on from whom to receive little children so that they
might grow rich in the delights of childbirth. Men whose
wives, though fertile, have proved unable to bear
children in their home have often found a compatible 1255
character so that they could shore up their old age with
children. This is how important it is for the seeds to be
able to mingle together with the other seeds in
combinations suitable for procreation, the thick
complementing the watery, the watery the thick. It also
matters in this regard what nourishment is used to 1260
sustain life; for some things make the seeds solidify in
the limbs, other things make them grow thin and waste
away. It also matters enormously what method is used in
the performance of sensual pleasure; for wives are
usually thought to be more likely to conceive in the 1265
position adopted by wild animals and four-footed beasts,
because in this position, with breasts lowered and hips
raised, the seeds can take up their positions in the right
places. Nor do our wives have any need at all of
sensuous movements; for a woman prevents herself
conceiving and struggles against it if in her delight she 1270
thrusts away from the man's penis with her buttocks,
making her entire body floppy in sinuous
wave-movements.
This is because she diverts the furrow away from the
true location and direction of the plough, turning the
impact of the seed away from the plot. Whores are in the
habit of moving like this for their own reasons, to avoid 1275
frequent insemination and pregnancy, and at the same
time to make the sex itself more pleasing to men.
Obviously our wives don't need any of these movements.
Nor is it by divine intervention or due to the arrows of
Venus that from time to time a girl of inferior looks is
loved – for sometimes the woman sees to it, by her 1280
actions, her compliant ways and her bodily cleanliness,
that she finds it easy to get you accustomed to the idea
of spending your life with her. Furthermore, familiar
intimacy breeds love; for that which is beaten with
frequent blows, however lightly, is conquered in the 1285

79

nonne vides etiam guttas in saxa cadentis
umoris longo in spatio pertundere saxa?

course of a long period and begins to break down. Don't you notice how even mere drops of water falling onto rocks bore through the rocks eventually?

TITI LUCRETI CARI DE RERUM NATURA

LIBER QUARTUS

COMMENTARY

INTRODUCTION TO LINES 1 - 25

The book opens with a declaration of intent and an apologia for his use of verse in communicating Epicurean philosophy. The lines are also to be found at 1.926-50 (cf 3.806-18 = 5.351-63; 1.1021-7 = 5.419-29), and editors have often attempted to locate the 'true' place in the poem as opposed to the 'imperfect transposition' (cf Kenney ad 3.806-18, Costa ad 5.128-41, Boyancé 82-3, Schrijvers (1970) 27-8) Bailey, however asserts (iii.p 1178) that L may have intended the lines to stand in both places, 'meaning probably, when he revised the poem, to substitute a proem more in conformity with his usual type and probably containing the praise of Epicurus' (vol.2.pp 757-8, Prol. VII.30). The lines were read in both places in antiquity; nor need this occasion any surprise, given the enormous difficulty of cross-referencing from book to book in ancient texts (Bailey vol.i.163, Reynolds and Wilson 2). Furthermore a passage of enormous beauty and significance such as this surely deserves repetition - cf L's clarion call 1.146-8, repeated at 2.59-61, 3.91-3, 6.39-41. It is thus by no means certain that L. merely transferred the lines from Book 1 as a stopgap. (Bailey vol.i.p.165).

Two ideas are interwoven in this proem. Firstly, the originality of L's enterprise, secondly its purpose. 'His poetry is of secondary importance' declares Bailey (vol.ii p.757); and yet the 'primary' purpose behind the poetry is only declared after nine lines charged with Alexandrian allusions declaring the poet's hopes and aspirations to *poetic* glory and originality. The sequence of thought thus teases the reader with the language of hermetic, obscure poetics announcing a very un-Alexandrian public mission which totally subverts the poetry to a purpose outside itself. L's poem *is* original, and it *is* a technical *tour de force* to cast difficult philosophy into delightful poetry; and yet its originality rests largely on its refusal to espouse the Alexandrian poetic of *l'art pour l'art* (cf Clausen) thus setting up a tension between allusion and intent, form and content. (See further Schrijvers (1970) 27-47, Minadeo 42-3, Boyancé 57-68).

1   trackless terrain of the Muses: the collocation of *avia Pieridum* stresses that it is artistic originality to which L. lays claim - in his philosophy he is a faithful disciple of Epicurus (cf 3.3-4).

The Muses were known as *Pierides* from their association with Mt Pierus in Thessaly (cf West ad Hesiod *Theogony* 53). Clay 210 suggests that L.'s choice of Pieria rather than Helicon is a deliberate distinction between himself and other poets; 'the springs of this mountain have no name. The steps and song of dancing Muses cannot be heard there; on its slopes no shepherds pasture their sheep.' He also suggests a connection between Pieria and Epicurus' word *apeiria* used of the infinity of the Universe – L. aspires not merely to the well-trodden slopes of Helicon, but to Epicurean infinity. (cf how at 1.118 it is Helicon from which Ennius brought down his crown).

2-3 I love: L. takes personal delight in his poetry – cf 1.924-5, 3.28. His declaration is made not merely to 'stimulate the flagging Memmius' (P.M. Brown ad 1.927-8) but more especially an expression of that pleasure which is central to Epicureanism (cf Rist ch.6, Gosling and Taylor chs 18-20, Boyancé 294).

2 untouched springs: an old tradition associates water with poetry (cf Commager (1962) 11-12) and the motifs of untraversed paths and pure springs are particularly reminiscent of Callimachus (*Frag*.1.27-8 Pfeiffer; *Ep*. 28 (*A.P.* XII.43), 1-4; *Hymn* 2.112. cf Kenney (1970) 370, Brown (1982) 81. See Introduction to this section.

3 draw from them: on the meaning of *haurire* cf West 1965 271-80. A similar use of the word to express poetic inspiration occurs at 1.412-3, Hor. *Sat*.2.4.94-5.

3-4 new flowers...crown: 'The notion of crowning by the Muses recalls the tradition of symbolic gift-giving that began with Hesiod (*Theog*.30-1) and was continued by Theocritus...' (Kenney (1970) 371). More particularly, L. has already described how Ennius 'was the first to bring down from lovely Helicon a crown of evergreen leafage' (1.117-8), words charged with reminiscence of the proem of Ennius' *Annales*; L. provocatively asserts his originality in words which are anything but original, alluding to the encomuim which the poet traditionally bequeathes to his subject (cf Nisbet-Hubbard ad Hor. *Odes* 1.26.7) and setting it on his own head. (On the link with Ennius see further Waszink (1954) 250-1, Brown (1982) 81).

5 fields whence...no other: this rounds off what Paratore calls 'the typically Hellenistic *topos* of the *inventor*'

85

(Paratore (1960) 310). The genre of the didactic epos had a long history, beginning with Hesiod, taken up by Presocratic philosophers such as Parmenides and Empedocles (cf 1.716-33) and exploited to the full in the Alexandrian quest for originality of subject matter and virtuosity of style. The genre began to enjoy a new lease of life in L.'s own time, with Cicero's translation of Aratus' *Phaenomena*, the *De Rerum Natura* of Egnatius, the *Empedoclea* of Sallustius (cf Cic. *ad Q.F.* 2.10.3) and others. The novelty of the *DRN* is that it is the first didactic epos to expound Epicurean philosophy in Latin; and yet this is no dreary versification of récherche obscurities - the irony of L.'s claim is that he alludes to the claims of esoteric, hermetic Alexandrian literature and in the same breath eschews esotericism and the philosophy of *l'art pour l'art*; on the contrary, the 'elegance of the Muses' is prompted by very ulterior motives (6-25).

6-7   the tight knots of religious beliefs: L. openly specifies the therapeutic object of his poetry. His hostility to religion and its accompanying fear of life after death have been declared right from the start (1.63-5, 80-101) and are the motive force behind all the philosophical argument (cf Introduction to 26-53).

7   untie...knots: this image draws out a play on the word *religio* as being etymologically linked with *religare* (to bind). See West (1969) 96.

8   dark...light: for this contrast cf 1.136-48, on the difficulty of illuminating the obscure discoveries of the Greeks, 3.1-2 describing Epicurus as raising so bright a light in such darkness (cf 5.11-12). Light is used as a symbol of poetic clarity and also of philosophical truth (*naturae species ratioque* 1.146) dispelling the shadows of ignorance and fear. (For L.'s debt to Parmenides in this equation of light and truth cf Waszink 253).

8-9   coat everything: cf 13,407, 6.1188; *OLD contingo* 5.

9   elegance: for the full range of meaning of *lepos* see Classen 100-103. Notice how L. produces this elegance in claiming it - the emphatic alliteration of carmina..contingens cuncta lepore, the expressive vowel richness of musaeo contingens cuncta; all five vowels and a diphthong in the space of three words.

10   Nor does this seem...: What West ((1969) 125-6) calls 'the brutal prosiness of this line' is especially striking

after the elegance of 1-9, and yet part of L.'s virtuosity is precisely his ability to incorporate 'everything that comes to hand' (West, *ibid*) and his refusal to allow restrictive notions of poetic propriety to deflect him from that clarity of expression upon which his purpose depends.

10-17 purpose: L. outlines what has been called 'the ornamental or seductive theory of art' (Arragon 371). The unconverted are compared to sick children who have to be tricked into taking unpleasant medicine. For the analogy cf Plato *Laws* 659e-660a, Hor.*Sat*.1.1.25-6 (cf also Empedocles' description of the unconvinced as *nepioi* ('fools', a word often used of children) at Frag. 414 (KR), and notice how primitive man was also *nepios* until Prometheus rendered them intelligent (Aeschylus *Prometheus Bound* 443-4)). The force of the analogy rests in: 1) the reduction of opponents to the status of foolish children 2) the comparability between the one-to-one treatment of the doctor and the personal conversion of the reader by the poet, and 3) the stress on contact (see 17n) as the source of true perception.

Furthermore, notice that L. both asserts the use of poetry as an illusion and a deceit, and at the same time shatters any real illusion by his disclosure – the reader, unlike the child, is *told* that he is being tricked. This again is a source of consistency within the book, the syllabus of which is a detailed exposition of how we in fact come to see reality as it is by recognising illusions (324-461) and delusions (dreams 962ff, love 1037-1191) for what they are. At the same time it flatters the reader with the tacit assumption that he is mature enough to let himself be deceived in this way – notice how *tibi* (20) contrasts with the 'masses' who 'shrink back in horror'.

The literary implications of this passage are wide. There is a clear allusion to the old tradition of poetry as both truth and fiction, the two being indistinguishable to the poet and his audience (Hesiod *Theogony* 26-8, Solon 21, Pindar *Olympian* 1.28f, *Nemean* 7.20ff, Eur. *Her.* 1341-6, Callimachus *Hymn* 1.5-8) while the same poets may assert the truth of their words no less than L. (Hesiod *Works and Days* 10, Pindar *Ol*.13.52, *Nem*.1.18 Callimachus *Frag*.442); L. transforms this into the paradox that the deliberate use of deceit is necessary to

87

tell the truth.

The mixture of honey and wormwood is compared to the union of sour philosophy and sweet poetry in a novel variation of the common claim to produce work which is both *dulce et utile* (sweet and also useful); Arragon (p.388) points out that later on the roles are reversed, whereby it is the *ratio* of Epicurean philosophy which sweetens the ugly realities so vividly brought to life in the poetry (esp. the plague at the end of book 6). cf Schrijvers (1970) 35-6, Boyance 5.

11   Wormwood: cf 2.400, 4.124. A substance used in the treatment of sore throat (Celsus *de med.* 4.7.) and stomach ailments (*ibid.* 4.12), and proverbial for being beneficial yet disgusting.

12   trying...cups: a comic touch, highlighting the difficulty of administering medicine to reluctant children, and the need for several attempts (cups). In formal terms 'trying' corresponds to lines 23-4 below.

13   This line mirrors line 9: *contingens..lepore* becoming *contingunt...liquore.* 'The smooth l sounds fit the sweetness of the honey, the slow rhythm its viscosity' (Brown ad 1.938).

Notice how L. brings out the precise detail of the colour of the honey (yellow), a factor of importance in persuading the child to drink it!

14-15 prank..drink up: there is a nice irony in the doctor playing a practical joke on a child, when one would expect the child to be playing a prank on adults. *perpotet* (drink up) also has the sense of 'tope, carouse' (*OLD perpoto* 1.) and contributes to the comic effect with a suggestion that the little boy is drunk on wormwood - for a similar effect cf 1.260-1, West (1969) 6-7.

16   tricked..sickened: for the play of words between *decepta* and *capiatur* cf Ennius *Ann* 359, Virgil *Aen.*7.295 L. plays on a contrast rather than a correspondence between the two words. (cf Brown's edition of Book 1,p.xxxviii).

17   contact: in the text I have adopted Lambinus' second suggestion *tactu* for the MSS *atacto,* although most modern editors print the anodyne *pacto* of Heinsius. *tactu* is both emphatically alliterative and also strikes the key-note of physical contact which is the motif running through the whole book - from the arguments explaining

that sensation is entirely the result of contact with *simulacra* (images) right through to the spectacle of lovers mauling each other in blind infatuation (1076ff; cf 2.742!). The trick works only as far as the lips because only the lips are in actual contact with the honey.

17   <u>recover</u>: the unconverted are compared to the sick, just as later in this book the romantic lover is described as *saucius* (wounded), his love as a *rabies* (cf *OLD rabies* 1b); the fear of death makes man render himself sick with sorrow (3.933-4), just as religion crushes him prostrate (1. 62-3). The climax of this motif is of course the lengthy description of the plague which ends the poem with a vision of a 'diseased population, burning with an insatiable and self-destructive thirst, weary and uncertain' (H.S. Commager 113). 'As the fever destroys the body, fear destroys peace of mind' (Bright, 632). The sickness is analogical to the psychological sickness of the unconverted – L cannot argue that Epicureanism banishes sickness altogether, in view of the agony in which Epicurus himself died (D.L.X.22).

18-19 <u>is regarded as too sour</u>: *videtur* clearly implies 'seems, but is not really'. *tristis* is used elsewhere in this book of noxious smells (125) and unpleasant food (634), thus overlapping the sense of bitter medicine and the emotionally unattractive features of Epicureanism, on which cf Santayana *Three Philosophical Poets* 52-4.

19-20 <u>too sour...the masses</u>: yet a few years later Cicero claimed that Epicureanism had taken over the whole of Italy (*Tusc*.4.6-7), particularly among the uneducated who knew no better. Epicureanism had been known in Rome since at least 154 BC, and reached a peak of popularity in the late Republic, its a-political stance appealing to a generation disillusioned with the political scene. (cf Brown (1982) 77, Momigliano (1941) 150-1, Paratore (1973) 184-191). It may be that L. is exaggerating the unpopularity of his philosophy for two reasons: firstly, Epicurus himself claimed 'never to have sought to please the masses' (Usener 187); secondly, L. may be applying the literary *topos* of the select, exclusive audience being made privy to literature which is not for general consumption – cf most famously Horace *Odes* 3.1.1, Williams 49ff. (On the problem of Amafinius' work and its relationship to the *DRN* (Cic. *Tusc*.4.6-7) see Classen (1968) 113).

21-2   the Muses...honey: L. rounds off the analogy with a reference back to lines 1 and 9, a form of ring-composition to draw the proem towards its close.

23   your...you: the addressee of the *De Rerum Natura* is Gaius Memmius, a political figure with literary inclinations; when he was propraetor of Bithynia in 57 BC he had the poets Catullus and Cinna on his staff (cf Catullus 10 and 28). It is quite possible, however, that 'you' here indicates the reader, as personal references to Memmius become increasingly infrequent as the poem proceeds, somewhat similar to the disappearing Perses in Hesiod's *Works and Days*. On this cf G.B. Townend, 'The Fading of Memmius', *CQ* 28 (1978) 267-83). On Memmius, see further Pauly-Wissowa *RE* s.v. Memmius (8); *OCD*[2] s.v. Memmius (2).

23-4   to see if I could: reminds the reader of the doctors forlornly attempting to administer the medicine (12n).

24-5   grasping...feeling: the true Epicurean has both an intellectual comprehension of the philosophy and also an emotional commitment to it.

INTRODUCTION TO LINES 26 - 215

tactus enim, tactus, pro divum numina sancta / corporis est sensus...
('For touch, touch, I swear by the holy powers of the gods, constitutes bodily sensation' 2.434-5).

The Atomic theory postulates that everything which exists is made up of physical atoms, and that further all effects must therefore have atomic causes. This entails that all changes in physical and mental states must be caused by change and/or movement in atomic formation, and hence both perception of the physical world and also 'inner states' are reducible to objective changes at atomic level. On the one hand this theory is entirely common-sense, arguing that our sense experience is reliable, its shortcomings being explicable by reference to other sense-experience (cf 469-521nn); on the other hand it purports to explain all sense-experience with a theory of effluences such that all sense-data, including dreams and visions of the dead, are made up of atoms from the thing or person we seem to perceive, and that these effluences must enter the body to be perceived, since perception only occurs when 'soul' atoms are actually touched by the effluence (cf 3.381-95).

Epicurus' famous assertion that 'all perceptions are true' is fraught with difficulties, of course; in the simple sense 'All perceptions are real' – that is, all perceptions are reactions to a physical stimulation of the sense-organs, and not just imagined (which would be nonsense on the atomic theory) – the assertion makes sense but does not go far enough. Epicurus did not merely say that perception is real, he also said that perceptions are true but *alogoi* (irrational); again, in a restricted sense this merely asserts that our sense-organs accurately relay, like a camera, the sense-data which impinge upon them, without being in a position (*qua* mere sense-organs) to pass any judgement on them; in this form all *perceptions* are true, whereas our *judgements* derived from them may be true or false without impugning the veracity of the senses themselves. But Epicurus went further still, asserting that every perception is perception of a real object which is represented *in* the sense-datum exactly as it actually is in reality – which lands him in trouble with the square tower (353-63n). The reduction of all sense-experience to objective events is appealing but liable to the objections of inconsistency of effect: the same food may taste sweet to me but sour to you, although the atomic structure is the same: the same tower looks round from here but square from there, and so on. As there is no reason to prefer situation S1 from situation S2, it becomes impossible to decide whether the food is 'really' sweet or 'really' sour – or neither. Epicurus' response to this was to develop his theory of the mental structures with which we interpret the (true) evidence of the senses – in particular his notion of 'general concept' (*prolepsis, notities*) allows us to identify the four-footed barking beast on the hearth-rug as a dog because we have seen dogs before; this can lead us into false judgements if we jump to the conclusion that the four-footed beast is a dog before we notice the horns on his forehead (cf 462-8). There is still the fundamental problem of 'things in themselves'; the theory asserts that our sense-organs only make contact with images, effluences or, in the case of touch, with the outermost surface of things, never with the things themselves. Yet Epicurus is still prepared to infer both the existence and the nature of 'things in themselves' from this superficial evidence, L even asserting blatantly (258) that 'things themselves are seen'. When it suits, however, L reverts to a more restricted system of sense-perception, as in his explanation of how we come to 'see' Centaurs (724-48). In effect, Epicurus wants to have it both ways; to refute Scepticism with his explanation that optical illusions are caused by the 'false opinions of the mind' and not the inadequacy of the senses, but then to use the inadequacy of the *images* – their tendency to merge together, for example (741ff) – to refute the hard-line empiricist who would assert that if we see Centaurs they must exist. For more information see Rist chs 2,5; Taylor; for the wider problems of epistemology see (e.g.) Ayer *The Problem of Knowledge*.

26–53 As it stands in the MSS, this passage is a doublet.

26–44 recapitulates book 3; 45–53 seem to have been composed with the intention of joining book 4 to book 2, and so should be deleted as redundant in the final order of the books. That L intended to publish the poem in the order I, II, IV... is corroborated also, according to Mewaldt (1908) 295 by the sequence of topics in the Epicurean *Letter to Herodotus* where the 'doctrine of the images follows the Atomic principles, and the theory of the soul only comes after the doctrine of sensory perception'. Those who reject this argument are forced to adopt some version of Marullus' rearrangement of the lines (Bailey's Oxford text prints: 45–8, 26–43, 51–3, 44, omitting 49–50, although Bailey in his 1947 edition admits that there is no means of accounting for the dislocation on mechanical grounds.) An attempt to justify Marullus' rearrangement has been made by Canfora 63–77 who argues that L intended to merge the two proems together into one but died before he had done so, so that the rearrangement is 'what L must have had in mind'. Yet Canfora's article alleges that the prologue of book 5, 'which recapitulates all four preceding books, in the order in which we read them' proves his theory that L's prologues 'snowball' as the poem progresses. A glance at 6.43–6 will show that this is far from a summary of books 1–5, being a short summary of book 5 alone; and indeed 5.61–3 would suggest to the reader that book 4 is merely concerned to rebut the empirical argument for the continuation of life after death based on sense-experience of the dead in dreams. 'The fourth book is thus regarded as a pendant to the third, removing one objection to the thesis which it has established and contributing to the attack upon men's fear of death' (A.S. Cox, 12).

Thus the recapitulatory summaries of previous books make no attempt to be exhaustive – on the contrary, whole sections of the utmost interest and brilliance are left in total silence for the rest of the poem (e.g. 4.1058–1191). The objective in these prologues is to establish continuity and coherence quickly and skilfully and then to press on with new material in building up a cumulative picture which is comprehensive and convincing. There is no parallel for a repetitive, 27-line summary of all the ground covered so far. The reason why the argument of book 4 is three times (1.132-5; 4.33-9; 5.62-3) condensed into a theory to explain the appearance of ghosts is partly linguistic (L's word for 'image' (*simulacrum*) also means ghost; cf *OLD simulacrum* 4b) and partly pedagogical – ghosts serve both to arrest the attention of the reader and also to underline the coherence between books 3 and 4. The only sensible way to print the text is thus to bracket 45-53.

27-8 healthy union...torn apart: *compta vigeret* is contrasted, by virtue of its similarity of sound, with *distracta rediret*.

28 constituent parts: *ordia prima* is an alternative for *primordia* or *corpora prima* (cf 3.438) or *exordia prima* (3.380), all meaning 'basic components', i.e. atoms or groups of atoms.

29-30 relevance: explained in 33-41, as a mechanistic disproof of survival after death; book 3 contains 29 proofs of extinction at death – this book disproves an alleged counter-argument.

30 'images': *simulacra*, *imago* (52), *effigias* (42) and *figura* (42) are all used to translate Epicurus' term *eidola*, denoting the slender film-like images constantly peeling off the surface of things, causing vision when they enter the eyes, thought and dreams when they enter directly into the mind.

31 skins: *membranae* is a metaphor (*quasi*) to translate *humenes*, found in the fragments of the Epicurean Diogenes of Oenoanda (cf M.F. Smith *AJA* 74 (1970) 57-8). The word connotes physiological ideas made explicit later on in the analogy of the amnion or caul (59-60), the snake sloughing its skin (60-2) and the bark of the tree (51).

32 stripped: *dereptae* suggests stripping clothes from a body.
back and forth: a slightly misleading phrase, as L. must have recognised that visual images fly forwards towards the observer, not backwards or sideways; his account of thought however (779-817) demands that all manner of images be available in the air all the time, regardless of

93

their source.

fly: the verb *volitant* at once suggests ghosts; cf Virgil *Aen* 7.89, 10.641-2. That is why L. proceeds immediately to treat of ghosts without finishing the previous assertion that images are the source of vision.

33-41 See Introduction to this section. The images we see are indeed those of the dead, but were emitted from the body *before* death and are still travelling abroad. L. may have in mind the famous scene in Homer's *Iliad* (23.54-107) where the ghost of Patroclos appears to Achilles; see esp. Achilles' conclusion (103f): 'even in the house of Hades the life and image (*eidolon*) is something, although the mind is not there at all...' cf 'some part of us can be left surviving...' at 39 below.

35 light-lacking: *luce carentum* is a grandiose phrase suggesting the heroic dead of ancient times; cf Hesiod *Works and Days* 155, Homer *Iliad* 18.11, Virgil *Aen*.2.85, (Plato) *Axiochus* 365c. The phrase continues the light vs dark contrast from line 8; it introduces a paradox of *images* of men who lack *light*; and it evokes the very deadness of the men concerned by suggesting that they belong to the distant heroic past.

37 woken up: *excierunt* is stressed, coming at the end of a sentence and the beginning of a line; it represents the sudden jolt of waking after the dreamy *languentis saepe sopore*.

37-41 There is a danger...: cf the phrasing of 1.120-6, where L. mocks Ennius' belief in the Underworld and transmigration of souls.

37 Acheron: one of the rivers in the Underworld - see *OCD*² s.v. and cf Milton *Paradise Lost* 2.575ff.

38 ghosts: see *umbra OLD* 7. L. debunks the superstitions relating to the *umbra* as shadow at 364-78.

39 some part: cf Homer *Iliad* 23.103 (above, 33-41n). Propertius 2.34.53; 4.7.1. cf *quiddam* at 3.878.

41 each to their own: *sua quaeque* are usually juxtaposed in Latin; the wide separation here is expressive of the physical splitting up of the atomic compounds.

43 *mittier* is the archaic form of the infinitive (passive). surface skin: *cortice* is the MSS reading, emended by most editors to *corpore*; yet the MSS reading has a subtle soundness. The *simulacrum* occupies that part of a body which the bark occupies on a tree - yet nobody would deny that the bark is an integral part of the tree,

and any faithful image (*simulacrum*) of a tree would be of a tree covered in bark, not whittled clean. L. is thus here stressing the identity of the image and the object such that, at any moment, an object has an immeasurable number of images making up its outer surface, so that each image as it departs conveys an image of the image which follows it, and so on. We only ever *see* the bark, not the tree. In a similar vein *rerum* (Lachmann's conjecture for the MSS *eorum*) may be justified precisely because it is repetitious after *rebus* earlier in the line; the constant stream of virtually identical images slipping from the surface of things is thus verbally represented in the double use of the same word in a single line.

44 however dull his brain: cf 5.882. This is not a back-handed insult to the reader, but rather an encouragement (it is easy to understand) and perhaps also a provocation (the reader really *must* be stupid if he can't understand...).

46-8 how they differ: matter is made up of indivisible particles which have a vast range of different shapes; see Epicurus *Letter to Herodotus* 42, *DRN* 2.333-729, Rist 44-6. On the problem of how non-sentient atoms can create sentient beings cf Furley (1966) 24-5.

47 without compulsion...yet driven: one of the problems in the Atomic theory is the notion of free will. Democritus was a thorough-going determinist in his physics, yet regarded man as free to act as he wishes (cf Barnes 534-5), causing Epicurus' famous riposte (*Men*.134) 'it is better to follow the myths of the gods than to become a slave to the destiny of the natural philosophers'; and yet his answer to the problem, the theory of the Swerve (*clinamen*), examined by L. at 2.216-93, raises more questions than it solves. For a fuller discussion see Bailey 316-327, Rist 51-2.

52 appearance and form: the images preserve the colour and the shape of the object seen; cf 243.

53 *cluet* has the force of the Greek verb *kluein* (cf 449) 'to be spoken of' (cf Brown ad 1.119) and is a word L seems to have been fond of (cf *OLD* s.v.2); and yet Bailey mistranslates it 'it appears' and the Loeb translator ignores it altogether; a course followed in the present translation in despair of finding a convincing rendering in English.

54-89 The argument is *a fortiori*.
      Invisibly fine things move more easily than visibly thicker things.
      We see examples of substances leaving bodies.
      Therefore: Invisibly fine images must leave bodies. The inference of atomic behaviour from the visible world is universal in L - cf for instance 1.311-27; 2.112-41. It is of course essential for L's argument that the individual images be invisible, perception being aroused by a sequence of films (89); and the distinction between the 'dissolved' and the 'condensed' will be of significance in explaining the different senses - sight demands coherent images whereas smell does not.

54   obvious: picks up from 44 ('however dull his brain'), confirming the redundancy of 45-53.

56   heat: 'conceived as a corporeal substance' (Bailey). cf West (1975) 99 + n.2, discussing 3.432 where '*vapor* must be visible'. L may be thinking of the distorted currents of air above the source of heat.

58   shirts: a comic touch - in hot weather cicadas take off their shirts just like humans.

59   skins: L here uses the word *membranas* literally, having used it metaphorically at 31, thus drawing the proof out of the conclusion which anticipates it. (cf Classen 84).

61   we often see: as ever, L appeals to common experience.

62   scalps: *spoliis* usually connotes the spoils of war, or booty (*OLD* s.v.2). The 'rare sense' (Costa ad 5.954) 'fleece or skin' should not allow us to ignore the strong overtones of 'spoils'; a sense it also retains at 5.954 (*pace* Costa) - animals did not give up their skins to early man without a fight.

64   things: for the repetition *rebus...rerum* cf 44n.

67   bodies: *corpora* suggests replicas of the thing itself, but 'tiny' does not mean that they are smaller than the source in shape and outline, merely that they are wafer-thin. (One of the classic objections to Epicurus' theory was the improbability of the image of an elephant being able to enter the human eye).

68   thrown off: the component atoms of a body are always vibrating internally against each other (πάλσις) (cf Diogenes Laertius X.50, Bailey 407); this jostling occurs throughout the body, but only those atoms on the surface can escape easily since those further inside are pushed back by those nearer the surface.

70-1 marshalled...: the imagery here is both archaic (*indupediri* being an old form of *impediri*) and military; the atoms on the surface are compared to soldiers in the front line of fighting; see OLD *frons* 6a, *locus* 2a, Sallust *Cat.* 59.5.

72 prodigally: *ac largiri* (Lachmann) has been adopted in the text for the meaningless *aciergiri* (OQ). The suggestion of 1 31, *ac iaculari*, is attractive – the repetition of *iacere...iaculari* representing the relentless flow of particles is highly appropriate – but is too far from the MSS reading to be explained palaeographically.

74 colour itself: the images are both 1) similar to the radiation of colour when light shines through a coloured screen and also 2) coloured themselves, insofar as we see things in colour. The case of colour in the Theatre is thus both analogous and organic to the argument.

75-83 theatres: L probably is thinking of wooden theatres, as the first stone theatre was constructed in 55 BC. Awnings were first used in 78 BC. cf 6.109, Prop.3.18.13; 4.1.15. On this whole passage cf West (1969) 38-41.

79 magnificence of the masked actors: a famous crux. The MSS read *patrum matrumque deorum*; and yet parents and gods are alike irrelevant here. We have seen the audience in *consessum* (78) and are now looking down on the *scena*. One attractive idea is to see in *deorum* a corruption of *deorsum* (Bergk, Bernays, Martin); in emending the line Richter (54) proposes *pulcram variamque deorsum*, drawing on Lachmann's suggestion *pulcram variamque decorem* and comparing line 983. He rejects *decorem* as tautologous and less attractive than the 'factually significant *deorsum*'. Yet we have already had the notion of 'below' in *subter* (78); and the conjecture of K. Müller in his recent edition (Zurich 1975) *personarumque decorem* (adopted in the text here), while palaeographically difficult to explain, avoids tautology of any sort and creates the vivid and impressive spectacle of colour being transmitted on to moving, masked actors. (for *persona* in this sense cf 297, Martial 3.43.4).

82 beauty: '*lepos*... denotes a beautifully colourful, shining brightness and appealing (*smiling*: 2.502...) pleasantness...' (Classen 101). For the image of surfaces laughing cf 1.8; 3.22.

85 emit...emit: the repetition of the word drives home the

factual correspondence of the phenomena.

87 **definite**: 'Because nature is bound by a contract, each phenomenon is mathematically predictable and predetermined. Hence the frequent use of the word *certus*:...' (Bergson 50) – but see 47n. L often links *certus* with *cerno* (I perceive); i.e. we have reliable senses (cf 473–8: 759–61; 766–7).

89 **discrete**: the individual images cannot be seen any more than individual stills can be seen when a cinema film is being shown; in both cases the sequence is too rapid (cf 105–6).

90–97 elaborates the distinction already drawn between scattered and condensed effluences; the effluences which do not cohere to form an image are drawn from deep down and are torn apart on their way out of the body.

90 **smell, smoke...**: L stresses the multiplicity of these effluences by his use of asyndeton.

91–3 **pour...cut to pieces**: the imagery changes from that of liquids (*diffusae abundant*) to solid objects being put through something like a cheese-grater. (cf the description of death at 3.531).

93–4 **journey...marching**: L seems to be suggesting the movement of soldiers – *contendo, coorior* are both commonly associated with military activity.

95 **surface colour**: obviously we do not see colour other than that on the surface of the object. For *membrana* cf 59n.

96 **tear it**: *discerpere* is elsewhere used (2.829) of 'unpicking' cloth.

97 **front line**: cf 71n.

98–109 **mirrors**: the reflection in mirrors of objects held up to them is a classic Epicurean proof of the existence of images. See 150–4,269–323, Diogenes of Oenoanda NF 5 and 6 (discussed in Laks and Millot 349–53). Notice here again how L's use of the technical term *simulacra* rather pre-empts the conclusion it is supposed to support (101).

98 **mirrors, water...any bright surface**: a nice use of the powerful tricolon figure – in 1) mirrors, 2) water...in fact 3) in *any* bright surface. Notice also the asyndeton of *speculis in aqua*, and the chiastic arrangement of *speculis...simulacra...simili specie*, a repetition reinforced by the doubling of *rerum* (100–101).

104 **accurate copies**: the MSS reading *formarum dissimilesque* makes no sense. Bailey's OCT reads *formae rerum similesque* although *forma* is elsewhere treated as an

98

attribute of the image, not a synonym for it (cf
51,69,87). Lachmann's *formarum illis similesque* is
awkward, requiring us to construe it *illisque similes*. The
most elegant – if palaeographically difficult – emendation
is Lambinus' *consimilesque*, adopted here *faute de mieux*.

106   constant quick: the images bounce off the mirror as fast
as they leave the object – Epicurus speaks (1.49f) of a
rheusis suneches...okeos (constant stream...swiftly).

108-9 nor...any other: L defies the reader to provide a
convincing alternative explanation.

110-28 The thinness of images. L picks up the point made at
105-6 (the invisibility of individual images) and now
attempts to convince us of the rationality of believing in
things we cannot see. As often, he offers examples from
the physical world, the first of which is an analogy – the
soul of a gnat (say) is made up of atoms of microscopic
size, but is not itself an image or effluence. The second
case is an example – the olfactory perception of invisible
scent has the same physical explanation (effluences) as
visual sense-experience – but the sequence of thought is
obscured by the lacuna in the text.

110   Come now: for the peremptory *nunc age* addressed to the
reader cf 1.265; 2.335, 731.

111-3 L launches into a contorted sentence to convey the idea
of a sliding scale of in/visibility. The elusiveness of the
meaning successfully creates exactly the 'now you see it,
now you don't' effect he is describing.

116-22 L is no more specific than 'living things' in describing
the microscopic organism, leaving the imagination free to
supply a precise referent; although the mention of three
parts may suggest insects with head, thorax and
abdomen. On this passage cf West (1969) 19.

116-7 This sentence is translated as a consecutive, requiring
the insertion of *ut* at the end of 116. This is both less
drastic than Purmann's *quorum* and clearer in sense.

118-22 L breaks up the lines into a series of staccato
questions, repeatedly prodding the reader somewhat in
the manner of satire (cf e.g. Juvenal *Sat*.1.51-2; Persius
*Sat*3.19-20). Notice also the anaphora of *quid* and the
alliteration of *praeterea primordia, quantula...quid
...quaeque*.

119   ball: *globus* represents of course an assumption on L's
part of the spherical nature of the tiny heart, although
the thrust of the passage denies the possibility of

knowing this. Elsewhere the word is only used of the sun and moon (5.69,472,665,720,722) – it is as if L is giving us a glimpse of the microscopic world in which the invisible eye of an insect becomes a telescopic glowing orb. cf 129–42n.

120-1 spirit and mind: all living things are endowed with spirit (*anima*) by definition – spirit is simply the 'life' which they lose at death, in common with man.

124 Catholicon: *panaces* is virtually a transliteration of the Greek *panax*, identified by *OLD* as a type of Opopanax (which certainly has the required degree of malodour).
wormwood: cf 16n.

125 Southernwood: *Artemisia fragrans*, used medicinally for complaints ranging from coughs to restricted urine. (Pliny *HN* 21.21.160).
centaury: named after the centaur Chiron (teacher of Achilles; cf Ovid *Ars Am*.1.11–12) who is said to have discovered its medicinal uses.

126-7 There is evidently a gap here, probably caused by the loss of a whole page of the archetype; this means that 52 lines are missing (Munro II.27–8). The translation attempts to finish off the sense of 123–6.

127-8 L rounds off the (missing) section with the *a fortiori* flourish that:
    1) individually invisible images are leaving bodies all the time
    2) we know of the existerᵤe or things we cannot see
  ∴ 3) how many more images must there be than we can see.

128 powerless: these 'ghosts' are as impotent as the *amenena karena* (strengthless heads) of the ghosts in Hades (Homer *Odyssey* 11.49).

129-42 'There is no doubt that this paragraph does to some extent interrupt the natural sequence of thought' declares Bailey. Lachmann, Bernays and Munro bracket the passage, Brieger put it after 109. It is however difficult to imagine an interpolator capable of writing it, and in any case the 'sequence of thought' is bound to remain something of a mystery in view of the lacuna of probably 52 lines after 126. The paragraph is, furthermore, a nice example of the way L can switch from the microscopic to the telescopic without warning, a sudden change of view-point being an asset to the didactic power of the work. In this passage L is tilting against the 'evidence' for heavenly monsters by explaining that the appearances we see may often be merely accidental combinations of discrete images into compound images (cf Epicurus *Letter to Herodotus* 48). The passage thus serves two purposes: it reassures the reader that the notion of flying figures is not so strange after all, and it also adds ammunition to the war against superstitious beliefs. The disproof of Centaurs is picked up again at 732-48 (in phenomenological terms) and at 5.878-924 (in zoological terms).

130 objects: *rebus rerum* evokes the constant stream of images peeling off things (cf 44n).

131 spontaneously: raises questions of causation - see 47n - but here simply means 'without any (divine) cause'.

132 this part of the sky: i.e. in the lower sky, that which we can see clearly, as opposed to the higher air of *aether*.

133 borne aloft: an epic-sounding phrase, building up to the mock-epic of 136-40 (cf similarly 2.206ff).

135 staining: a surprising word (*violare*) to use of white clouds - but cf 3.20-1 where white snow 'stains' the abode of the gods.

136 caressing: Bailey compares Cicero's translation of Aratus *Phaenomena* 88 'caressing the fire-bearing aether with their quivering wings'.

136-40 The images are surrealistic, the language is epic; this is perhaps overstated to convince the reader that compared with these outrageous spectacles, the theory of images is perfectly plausible. Tales of the Gigantomachy or Battle of the Giants were well-known (see *OCD²* 'Giants'). The mention of massive mountains may call to mind the tale of Otus and Ephialtes mounting Pelion upon Ossa (Graves vol.i.pp 136-8), the ripping of rocks from mountains may recall Hesiod *Theogony* 674-5 on the battle of the Titans 'with steep rocks in their sturdy hands' (see West's note to 617-719 on the Titanomachy). The 'monster' may in that case suggest the hundred-handed creatures which supported Zeus and the Olympian gods against the Titans (Homer *Iliad* i.396-406, Hesiod *Theogony* 711ff) when summoned by Thetis. Notice the heavy alliteration (*volare videntur...magni montes...solem succedere*) and the emphatic repetition *montes...montibus.*

141-2 There is no need to transfer these lines to follow 133 (135), as Lambinus, Bailey (OCT) and others have. The grammatical difficulty of supplying a referent for the neuter plural *liquentia* is as nothing compared with the logical difficulty of understanding the word before clouds have been mentioned. The pair of lines rounds off the short digression, returning from the clouds to the *simulacra. liquentia* may simply be a summing up: 'all these things'.

143-75 The rapidity of formation of the images.

143-67 Works up to the instant reflection of images over vast distances, analogous to the rapidity of movement of the light of the sun. In 168-75 the rapidity with which a clear sky becomes stormy shows *a fortiori* the enormous rapidity of the movement of the images.

143 facility...: the triad of adjectives *facili...celeri...perpetuo* is matched by the triad of verbs *fluant...lapsaque cedant.*

144-5 Lacuna marked by Lachmann. The obvious sense to be supplied is 'I will explain', most easily conveyed by inserting 2.66, as M.F. Smith suggests.

146-7 The thought behind this passage is clear, if the text is not. There are three types of surface for images to encounter; transparent, opaque and reflecting. The last two are precisely described (*aspera...splendida*) but the first is left with the limp *alias* - 'What "other things"?' asks Bailey. The corruption here may stem from a corruption in 147, where *vestem* can hardly stand. Cloth is only exceptionally diaphanous, and would thus be a lamentable example to put *in primis*. The best solution is undoubtedly Oppenrieder's *vitrum*, 'emended' to *vestem* by a scribe who thought L was still thinking of clouds (which may pass through cloth but not˙ glass), as suggested by Richter (56). It would then follow that whoever changed *vitrum* to *vestem* then changed the text elsewhere to suit cloth but not glass. Richter suggests emending *alias* to *liquidas* - which is nowhere attested in *OLD* with the meaning 'transparent' - or the insertion of a line to fill in the sense of *alias* with the precision we need. The final text conveys the identical movement of all images through the air until they meet objects other than themselves, when their fate depends on the nature of the obstacle, and it provides exactly the word (*limpida*) needed to balance *aspera* and *splendida*.

148 chopped: the clash of ictus and accent in *ibi iam* well suggests the chopping movement. Notice also the wry

irony of the wood doing the chopping in this case!

153 <u>without needing to be reminded</u>: L often endows his physical phenomena with human attributes; cf 188,244-5,317,429,822.

154 <u>flow</u>: *redundent* picks up *abundat* from 145.

155-6 <u>the image appears</u>: the suddenness of the reflection is admirably conveyed in the staccato *apparet imago* coming after the stream of relative terms.

157-8 the enjambment suggests the interminable flow of the images; and the repetition *tenuis tenuisque* conveys the identical sequence. Thus the chiastic arrangement of line 158 leaves *texturas* and *figuras* enclosing the rest; *textura* denotes a 'web' of atoms knitted together, *figuras* is the end result, a representation of the shape of the object – thus we first see the trees, then the wood, in the sequence in which the process occurs. cf 6.776.

159 <u>great...short</u>: the juxtaposition of *multa brevi* is deliberate, as in 161.

164 <u>a moment of time</u>: time appears to be split into atoms just like matter – cf 794-5n.

165 <u>great...many...all...everywhere</u>: a forcible string of near-synonyms to emphasise the point. cf. 5.1002.

166 <u>everything</u>: *omnis* is Voss' conjecture for MSS *oris* which is very weak ('to the outlines' glosses Bailey – although it is real things, not mere outlines, that the mirror reflects; his 'parallel' 142 is exactly the opposite – clouds do not *become* Giants, they merely resemble them, whereas here it is *res*, not *species*, that are at work) *omnis* is close to 242, the eyes there performing the same feat as the mirror here. Both passages also have an effective enjambment which suggests the swiftness of the images in the lack of a pause between lines (cf Townend 338. 'There is clearly a tendency...for some sort of pause to be expected at the end of a hexameter').

167 <u>everything answers</u>: *res...respondent* makes better sound than science, since elsewhere L asserts that we do not see *res* but only images; clearly we must not push 'answer' beyond a metaphorical significance, 'similar shape and colour' referring obviously to copies and not originals.

168-9 <u>weather</u>: this epic storm begins suddenly; *tempestas* taken backwards with *liquidissima* merely means 'weather', but its position leads right into the sudden storm; as if the storm has broken before the poet has had a chance to put a noun to *liquidissima*.

170 Underworld: as if the world has been inverted, the 'caverns of the sky' becoming the caverns of the Underworld and vice versa. See 6.536-42, West (1969) 25-6.

173 faces of dark fear: a vivid metaphor, expressive of the colour of the sky and the terror it inspires, even in a poet so in love with nature. (cf West (1969) 58; Gillis 354).

174-5 how tiny: *a fortiori* again, dependent on the principle that speed of formation is in inverse proportion to size: explained 183ff.

176-215 Rapidity of motion of the images.

176 come now: cf 110n.

179 inclinations: MSS read *numine*, as do most modern editors. At 3.144 *numen* and *momen* are juxtaposed as if 'inclination' and 'impulse' are seen in hendiadys as virtually the same thing. No need therefore for Marullus' *momine*.

180-2 verses: =909-11. The lines are an Alexandrian *topos*; cf Antipater of Sidon 47,7 (*AP* 7.713.7-8), Asclepiades (*AP* 7.11) - L., like the Alexandrian poets, professes a poetic of quality over quantity, sweetness over bombast. See Brown (1982), Kenney (1970) 371-2.

181 swan: see Otto, s.v. *cycnus* 2. For this sort of comparison of bird-song cf Theocritus 5.136, Pindar *Olympian* 2.87-9, and notice how L applies it to himself and Epicurus at 3.6-7.

187 beaten: *cuduntur* is an expressive verb, picked up by *plaga* in the next line.

189-90 light...light: for the polyptoton of *lumine lumen...fulgere fulgur*, suggestive of the unbroken chain of light and flashes, cf Brown (1983) 158-60.

190 team: *protelum* is a row of beasts of burden harnessed together. The juxtaposition with *stimulatur* is expressive - these 'beasts' are being goaded into movement like real beasts.

192 stupendous: the very length of *immemorabile* suggests the vast distance it describes.

193-4 tiny little impulse: the lightness and fine texture of the images as factors conducive to high speed have excited no surprise, but many editors feel that a 'tiny force' is less likely to produce high speed than a massive horse-power, and have attempted to construe *parvula* with *simulacra* - which leaves *causa* hanging limply. The whole phrase *parvula causa...procul a tergo* must be understood as a unit, whereby *parvula causa procul a tergo* does produce high speed *immemorabile per spatium*, kinetic force being cumulative, not constant, according to L (cf 6.340-2 for the 'snowballing' theory of speed). A certain paradoxical wonder informs the idea that so tiny a charge as the nudge of an atom can snowball into a flood of energy as powerful as the sun, especially since the whole topic of atomic movement raises epistemological questions highly relevant to this book. (cf 2.308-32, Bailey 332). *parvula* is thus provocative rather than concessive – pointing to the paradox of kinetic theory which converts minute energy and massive distance into high speed.

198 intervening air: the fifth-foot spondee (as in 187) may suggest the floating movement of the image through the air.

199-203 is the premiss from which the *a fortiori* conclusion (204-8) is drawn, although L offers no evidence for his assertion that sunlight is drawn from 'deep inside' the sun.

201 day: an apposite reminder that it is the alternation of sunlight and darkness which defines 'days'.

203 fly...flood: one expects flying to be in the sky, flooding to be from the sea to the land; L neatly turns our perspective upside-down to see things from the sun's point of view.

211 water: L seems to be imagining a shallow tray of water put under the open sky. The principle of mirrors has been explained at 98-109, and receives further treatment at 269-323.

212-3 stars...: notice the hushed s alliteration of these lines (cf Virgil *Aen*.4.81), the vocalic richness and assonance, and the gentle liquids of: extemplo caelo stellante...

215 the shores of the earth: like *in luminis oras*, an Ennian phrase found at 5.224 (see Costa *ad loc*), 1.22; there is more than a touch of grandeur in the periphrasis.

INTRODUCTION TO LINES 216 - 822: SENSATION

26-215 have given the reader the theory of images and effluences required to understand the mechanics of perception. L now proceeds to deal with: 1) Sight (216-521) 2) Hearing (522-614) 3) Taste (615-72) and 4) Smell (673-705). 722-822 deals with thought. L nowhere deals separately with touch, presumably since his theory of perception reduces all the senses - and thought also - to touch (2.434-5; cf 265-8n).

In his analysis of perception, L tackles all the hard problems raised by scepticism (324-468) and science (the dense passage on mirrors (269-323) draws on considerable interest in the phenomenon in the ancient world; on the study of 'catoptrics' see Annas and Barnes 73). In particular, the long catalogue of optical illusions (387-468) is taken almost entirely from the works of the Sceptic philosophers (see nn), and shows us L bearding the lion in his den, confident that for all the artistry of the problems, he can overcome them. This is, furthermore, an index of the universal nature of L's enthusiasm; our senses *can* deceive us, and these deceptions are a wonderful part of the world to be explored and explained.

216*7 *mira* (OQ) requires the postulation of a lacuna after 216; there is furthermore an abrupt break in thought from the speed of the images to the common origins of the senses touch, taste and hearing. The position is complicated by the fact that 216-29 are repeated almost identically at 6.922-33, leading at least one scholar (Richter 60-1) to argue that they are interpolated here by an intelligent reader who realised the lacuna after 216 and noticed that 217 = 6.922; he therefore thought to plug the gap in 4 with what he saw as a repetition of the lines in 6. (cf Müller, *Philologus* 102 (1958) 273) Richter is right to point to the eccentricity of 218-29 at this point, when we are concentrating on sight to the exclusion of the other senses, which only come under scrutiny at 522ff; and yet the lines were read in both books in antiquity (see Munro ad 4.218), leaving open the possibility that L himself did the 'interpolating'. There is certainly a lacuna in the text, and the break in the sequence of thought suggests that a whole section is missing. 218-29 may be interpolated, but they are not ludicrously out of place here, in the way they describe in general terms the many different effluences flying abroad; L first states the common cause of all perception, before going into specific detail about the differences between the senses.

219 cold..heat..spray: cold and heat are not visual (but cf 56n), which underlines the identity L is seeking to establish between visual and non-visual sense-experience.

220 gnaws away: *exesor* is a word which only occurs here. The idea is reminiscent of the earlier proofs of the atomic theory which pointed to gradual erosion: 1.311-21. The word also 'reminds us that the sandstone walls near the sea do come to look as though creatures had gnawed at them' (West (1969) 11-12).

221 flying: perhaps a reference to Ennius' *Epigrammata* 18 (V³): *volito vivus per ora virum* ('I live flying through the mouths of men').

224 wormwood: cf 11n. Notice how *tangit amaror* hits the reader as a sudden sharp phrase, after the enjambment of *diluta..absinthia*; the evocative effect is deliberate.

229 see...smell...: notice the simultaneity of all the senses brought out by the asyndeton of this line. 'At any time' may seem overstated, but cf 3.112-6 for receptivity during sleep.

230-8 We recognise a shape in the dark by touching it.
We recognise the same shape in daylight by looking.
∴ Looking is a form of touching, i.e. contact with the images.
The syllogism is hardly watertight, and is only tenable here since the conclusion has already been accepted before the premisses are even stated. I may realise that there is a dog next door by hearing it bark or by seeing through the window, but the only common ground between the two sense-experiences is that they are both sense-experiences; which leaves L with the jejune conclusion that perception is perception.

231-3 The hard c alliteration of these lines is surely deliberate, suggesting the firm outlines of the shape.

232 similar: not identical, since sight only meets effluent images, whereas touch meets the object itself.

235 darkness..light: *in tenebris* is deliberately juxtaposed with *in luci*.

239-43 L, having declared (165) that images fly in all directions, now points out why we only see what we direct our gaze towards; the images which are radiating from objects are only visible when they meet our eyes. One has to understand the unspoken qualification to 240, viz that images only move in straight lines (unlike sounds and smells (595ff, 687ff)).

244-55   L now deals with the problem of how we manage to assess the distance between ourselves and the things we see by postulating that the images drive a channel of air in front of them; we feel the amount of air pushed through our eyes and judge distances from that. Bailey points out two obvious flaws with this theory; 1) elsewhere (196-8) L has asserted that the images are of such fine texture that they '..ooze through the intervening air'. 2) we have no sensation of air pushed through our eyes in fact - and without any empirical verification it is difficult to sustain this argument. One difficulty with Epicurus' theory of images which L fails to deal with is related to this topic: how is it that the image of, say, an elephant can enter the eyes, given its enormous size? L might have argued that our judgement of distance depends on image-size relative to object-size, but would then have had to explain how the image comes to be diminished in size while remaining a complete picture of the object. (cf Bailey vol iii p.1207-8).

246   shoves..drives on: *protrudit* suggests the initial shove, *agit* the steady motion from then on.

247   between: the order of words is expressive - *quicumque* is broken into two (tmesis), thereby also driving a wedge between the image (*se*) and our eyes (*oculos*), recreating in words the physical distance from object to eye and the channel of air (*cumque est* goes with *aera*) locked inbetween.

249   brushes: *perterget* occurs again at 252 and 277 - cf also 6.119 where 'that dry sound (thunder) grates on (*terget*) the ears'; the idea of 'touching while passing through' is prominent, rather than any idea of 'cleansing'. Presumably the air finds its own way out of the head again. L's language (*per..per-...per-..*) suggests that the eyes are a coincidental obstacle to be passed through.

251-3   A neat equation - the greater the distance, the more air.

254-5   at the same moment: the simultaneity of the two judgements - the nature and the distance of the object - is consistent with the almost incalculable speed of the images (176ff) but makes it difficult to see how we can distinguish the near from the far.

256-68   L attempts to explain how it is that individual images are imperceptible but things are still perceived, drawing analogies from wind and cold. The problem is both

practical - and as such already dealt with at 3.370-95 -
and logical; if one atom is imperceptible, then so are two;
if two, then three, if x-1, then x. This form of argument
was known as the Sorites (see now Barnes 'Medicine,
Experience and Logic' in *Science and Speculation*, ed.
Barnes, Brunschwig, Burnyeat and Schofield pp.24-68),
first appearing in Galen *Med.Exp.* XVII 1-3, and
produces such paradoxical conclusions as that a man with
a million hairs on his head is bald. L avoids getting
entangled thus, and concentrates instead on recognisable
sense-experience.

258 things themselves: strictly speaking we only see images
which are emitted not the things in themselves.

259 wind: strong v alliteration in this line - cf 1.271.

260-1 each separate particle: L emphasises the effect with the
three-word phrase culminating in the effective diminutive
particulam.

265-8 When we touch a stone we can *see* that it is surface
colour that we are touching, but we do not *feel* colour
but rather the hardness deep down. This example seems
unrelated to the two preceding ones, except insofar as
the hardness of the stone is composed of an incalculable
(and individually soft) series of atomic layers. It is
curious that L did not treat the sense of touch in more
detail (see Schoenheim 81ff); on the one hand touch is
the exception to the rule that perception depends on
atomic effluences, but on the other hand touch appears to
prove that *res ipsae* can be perceived directly, as must
be so in the present example: 'Effluences in their normal
form are out of the question, since the always extremely
subtle images just are not hard' (Schoenheim 85).

269 - 323 MIRRORS

269-91 L attempts to explain how it is that an object seen
in a mirror appears to be on the other side of the mirror - as
if the mirror were clear glass through which we see the
object. L's explanation rests on the 'air-channel' theory
already explained at 244-55: since the image travels double the
distance between ourselves and the mirror, it must shove
double the amount of air back to us, which will lead us to
suppose that the object is twice as far away from us as the
mirror is. Objections to the 'air-channel' theory have been
explained at 244-55n.

270 removed: Marullus' *semota* is the reading of Bailey, 'in view of *semota* 288'. Yet if a parallel is all that is needed, one need only compare 305; no need therefore to emend *remmota*.

271 reliably: L distinguishes the mendacious sense-appearance of the mirror image from the reliable perception of things seen through an open doorway; the problems of sensory illusion will be fully dealt with 324ff.

274 double, two-part: Bailey and Munro see this as pure tautology, without any special point: in fact, the line is carefully constructed, *is...visus* enclosing the 'tautologous' phrase just as the perception itself is seen as consisting in a double (physically tautologous, if you like) air-channel.

276 doors: Roman doors were usually double doors.

279 the image of the mirror: this clearly refers to our perception of the mirror itself – the image reflected by the mirror only reaches us at 284. Thus the order of perception is: 1) air 2) mirror 3) air 4) image reflected off the mirror.

284 in exactly the same way: the MSS reading *in eum* is surely wrong – there is no evidence for a masculine form *speculus*; nor does there seem much point in *idem* adopted by Bailey, Munro and others. The point of the line is that the motion of the two images (that of the mirror and that of ourselves) occurs in the same way at the same time, which makes Howard's *itidem* (*Classical Philology* 56 (1961) 152-3) the most attractive emendation.

285 returns to our eyes: not that we have *seen* the image before; but there is a nice irony about the image *of* our eyes leaving our eyes and then being reflected back *into* our eyes.

292-301 The reversal of left and right in mirror images.

295 not...unharmed: the back becomes the front, without turning the image sideways through 180 degrees, as would be necessary to preserve the original sides. Remember that the image is three-dimensional, the prominent parts of the body emitting their 'images' earlier than the rest, causing these 'prominent' images to hit the mirror first and turn first – thus the parallel of the mask is perfect.

296-9 eliditur...adlidat...elisam: the repetition underlines the exact analogy of the mask and by the physicality of the word stresses the violence of the apparently effortless

110

process of reflection (notice also L's earlier use of *incolumis* (unharmed) 295).

98-9 possibly: the MSS reading *fronte* is adopted by many editors but lacks conviction – Bailey's gloss 'straight in its front' only obfuscates the meaning. The *Codex Vaticanus* (*A*) read simply *forte*, and this – for all its dullness – is more likely to be right.

99-347 The MSS O and Q have 299-322 and 323-347 in the wrong order, suggesting that a leaf of the archetype had fallen out and been replaced the wrong way round.

00 both: *ut* appears twice in this line in the MSS, justified by many editors in view of the 'intervening clause' (Bailey). The repetition can be paralleled in e.g. Cic. *ad Att.*3.5.8, Plaut. *Pseud.*579ff, *Amph.*495, but it remains awkward. The first *ut* is correct, supported by the parallel *fit ut* in 293, just as *recta* is picked up by *rectam.* (295-298), *eliditur* by *elisam* (296-9), *retrorsum* by *retro* (295-9). I have tentatively printed *et* in place of the second *ut*, to set up a 'both..and' phrase picked up and completed by the *et* in the next line – both the right becomes left and the left becomes right.

00-1 right...left: notice the 'mirror-image' reversal in the order of words – *dexter'...sit² laevus³...laevo³ sit²...dexter'.*

02-10 If one mirror reverses the image, then two mirrors must restore the 'real' arrangement; such that any odd number of mirrors will reverse, any even number of mirrors restore the image.

02 mirror to mirror: the verbal repetition again expresses the sequence of mirrors used.

03 even six: Many editors emend the MSS reading here to *sexve* (Marullus, Munro, Bailey (OCT)) or *aut sex* (Lachmann, M.F. Smith, Martin, Bailey (1947)); but Ernout is surely on the right lines to see it as expressive asyndeton, suggestive of the unexpected appearance of the image in mirror after mirror – the MSS reading better shows the excited astonishment of the poet: 'five, even six...'.

04-6 labyrinthine: the phrasing of these lines – in particular the unique adverb *torte* – well suggests the myth of the Labyrinth of Crete in which the minotaur was kept, from which Theseus effected an exit only with the aid of Ariadne.

308 **shine through:** *translucet* elsewhere means 'to be transparent, let light through' (*OLD* s.v.2), bringing us neatly back to the comparison with the doorway *through* which images pass.

309-10 The phrasing is deliberately confusing, to suggest the instantaneous flipping from left to right and back.

311-17 Concave mirrors preserve the true arrangement of sides. For illustration of the process, see Bailey (1947) vol.3.p.1218. The first of L's reasons for this phenomenon is a plausible extension of the principle just enunciated, viz. that a concave mirror acts as a double mirror which reflects twice. The second is more fanciful, arguing that the image is spun round in ricochet off the curved side of the mirror.

317 **teacnes:** for the personification cf 153n.

318-23 Mirrors reflecting movement. L builds again on the idea of our perception consisting of a series of static images – something like a cartoon film – which when 'played' in rapid succession, give the appearance of movement. The stream of *re-* words in lines 321-3 suggests this constant succession of almost identical images.

322 **equal angles:** the editors sagely remark that the angle of reflection is equal to the angle of incidence – but it may be that, since L is describing movement by the subject sideways across the mirror, he means no more than 'directly opposite the subject'.

324-78 Problems of vision. L now begins what is philosophically the most important part of the book. He has explained the mechanics of perception; now he must attempt to persuade us that the senses are reliable, in the face of a long tradition of Scepticism. (See Introduction to 469-521).

324-31 L's first point is simply to refer to the vulnerable nature of the sense-organs; gazing into the sun can damage the eyes. (Sextus Empiricus *OP* 1.45 refers to the way gazing into bright light distorts our perception subsequently of the letters in a book: L does not wish to introduce this topic of distortion until 332).

326 **from high heaven:** *alte* goes with *graviter* (heavily), in accordance with his theory of dynamics (cf 193-4n). The word also suggests 'deeply', i.e. boring deep into the eyes. Notice furthermore how L stresses the '*clean* air' (no collisions en route to diminish the impact) and how

the motion (*feruntur*) is assonant with the force (*feriunt*).

330-1   fire...breed: notice the paronomasia of *ignis- gignunt*, suggestive of the physical link between the fire and the production of pain.

331   work their way in: *insinuando* is poised at the end of the sentence, suggesting the end of the process as the unpleasant sensation of fire working its way into the eyes.

332-6   The argument from jaundice appears also at Sextus Empiricus *OP* 1.44 - neither he nor L seem to know that it is simply not true that things look yellow to the jaundiced. Nor is L's example sustained without treason to his own theory; Epicurus had insisted that the images enter our bodies without any disturbance from our own effluent images (*Hdt.* 49) L's idea of 'seeds of yellowness' meeting the images is thus rampant heresy. (cf Schoenheim 79). His final point is perhaps more consistent with Epicurean theory - that the yellowness is like tinted contact-lenses which impart their colour to the images as they pass through.

337-52   L attempts to explain how it is that we can see objects which are in the light when we are in the dark, but not vice versa. To do so he postulates two different sorts of air - light and darkness being properties of air, which is material (the alternative being non-existence) and hence productive of material reactions in other matter. Dark air blocks up the eyes, light air cleanses them, so whichever of the two is the last to enter the eyes will be the predominant force. The contrast of dark and light is stressed, especially by the switch from p alliteration in 339 to q/c alliteration in 340.

341   cleans: for the idea of air as a cleansing force in the eyes cf *perterget* 249.

344   passages of the eyes: *vias oculorum* must be the passages in the eyes, not the way to the eyes, as Bailey asserts. We already know the state of play outside the eyes, and the motion to the eyes is irrelevant here - what matters is the effect *inside* the eyes. Compare 350 *foramina* which clearly refers to the apertures in the body.

344-7   The tenses clearly show the sequence of events. First the blockading (pluperfect *obsederat*), then the filling with light and opening the roads (perfects *replevit*, *patefecit*), finally the images follow in the immediate present tense (*sequuntur*) and sting us into sight.

352 <u>incapable:</u> the sluggish rhythm of this line well suggests the clogging of the eyes with the thick sludge o' darkness.

353-63 The square tower looks round from a distance. This was a classic weapon in the armoury of the Sceptic (Sextus Empiricus *OP* 1.32, *AM* 7.208, 414) and is not handled well by the Epicureans; L here at first attempts to explain the phenomenon with the theory of the sharp edges of the images being rubbed off in transit, but then tries to tell us that the tower does not *really* look round, except as a 'shadowy copy' of 'really' round things. L cannot deny that the tower looks round – but nor can he admit that it does without surrendering the fundamental veracity of the senses upon which Epicurean epistemology depends. (cf Annas and Barnes 105-6).

353 <u>from far off:</u> cf Plato *Philebus* 38ce, Euripides *Ion* 586-7, Descartes *Meditations* 6.

356-7 <u>force...impact:</u> L seems to be thinking in military terms of a spear flung at the enemy lines (*acies* may mean that as well as 'eyes') which however fails to reach its target: *perlabitur* (gliding) suggests the flying spear floating ineffectually through the air.

361 <u>rounded:</u> Bailey retains the MSS reading *tuantur* ('are seen as if') although conceding the difficulty of understanding *structa* twice; it is also difficult to accept *tuantur* as passive. Munro's *terantur* is far more convincing; it is used with exactly this sense in Pliny *N.H.* xxxv.193, and it perfectly expresses the apparent sanding-down of sharp corners to smooth curves as in *hebescere* (359).

363 <u>shadowy:</u> *adumbratim* plants the seed of 'shadows' (*umbra*) which L will deal with in the next section.

364-78 The argument now leaves sensory illusion for a few lines to deal with the phenomenon of our shadow which appears to follow us. This is partly to break up the long catalogue of illusions, partly because the shadow has excited superstitious beliefs in many societies (see 366n).

365 <u>imitate..gestures:</u> the phrasing is close to that of 319 describing the action of mirrors; L is concerned to underline the basic consistency of the mechanics of both.

366 <u>if you believe:</u> for fascinating accounts of superstitious beliefs regarding shadows see Frazer Part 2 ('Taboo') pp 77-90; it is interesting that he records similar fears related to the use of mirrors (*ibid* 94-6). L, after

ironically endowing the shadows with the power to 'follow our tracks...', demythologises the matter by reducing this magic shadow to the status of mere 'air devoid of light'; he then repeats the process (367-9).

370 fixed, specific: L is exact in his wording – the shadow moves only in fixed places and only in a fixed sequence.

376 wool being drawn into the fire: the instant disappearance of the shadow at the point of contact with the sunlight pouring onto the ground is compared to the instant combustion of the end of a piece of wool held over a flame.

378 washes away: cf how the 'light air' flushes out the black air behind the eyes (341).

379-86 The eyes are like a camera which records images without being in a position to judge their veracity; only the 'reasoning power of the mind' can do that.

381-2 the same..the same: effective anaphora, alluding to the popular (and false) belief that the shadow is 'something' which can retain an identity.

384 distinctions: 381-5 constitute a long, involved sentence, flooding the mind as the sense-impressions flood the senses, leaving only the mind to 'sift apart' (cf Kenney ad 3.363 on cernere) the truth amid the chaff.

387-90 L begins this catalogue of illusions with the familiar experience of the passenger on a moving vehicle believing that the stationary vehicles nearby are moving whereas his is stationary – though more common still is the belief that our own stationary vehicle is moving when an adjacent vehicle begins to move in the opposite direction. cf Cicero Acad.Prior. 2.25.81, Sextus Empiricus AM 7.414.

388 passing us by: praeter-ire is split (tmesis) by the insertion of creditur, expressive of the doubt in the passenger's mind – we are (I think) moving – and setting up a jerky rhythm appropriate to the movement. cf 390.

389-90 L caps this last assertion with a stronger, fantastic image of the hills and fields 'flying towards the stern'; such a ludicrous belief, he implies, is really no more surprising than the earlier sensation in 387-8.

391-6 Distant stars seem to be stationary when we know that they are moving; cf Sextus Empiricus OP 1.118; 107. L's account is stylish – notice the paradox of stars fixed in caverns, the juxtaposition of obitus exorta forcing these 'stationary' stars to set and rise in the switch of a word, the poetic conceit of stars 'pacing out the sky'.

396 <u>the facts</u>: *res ipsa* merely indicates 'the world as we know it from *all* our experience'; it is the before-and-after knowledge which convinces us that the planets, like the hands of a clock, are moving.

397-9 *exstantesque* is grammatically difficult, and has either been emended (Lachmann's *exstant usque*) or explained away. Bailey is, however, right to see the sentence as something of an anacoluthon – the mountains float in glorious isolation in grammar as in life, only being drawn together into the structure of the sentence in 399 when we see them *coniunctis* to form an *insula*, the cohesion being underlined by the a-b-b-a pattern of *insula – coniunctis..ex his – una*, the whole crowned by the long-awaited word of recognition *videtur*. (For this free-wheeling construction cf 5.460-66.) Notice also the juxtaposition of plural and singular in *insula coniunctis*, merging the apparently discrete mountains into a single land-mass.

400-403 Dizziness makes the static appear to be moving.

400 <u>rotate</u>: the giddy spinning is well brought out by the assonance of cir<u>cumc</u>ursare columnae, the c alliteration, and the sound of ver<u>sari</u>..-cur<u>sa</u>re.

401-3 Notice the enjam<u>b</u>ment of <u>401-2</u>, the rapid rhythm of 401, and the poised postponement of *minari* suggesting that the children believe the roof *is* falling in...until it doesn't.

404-13 There is no obvious parallel to t<u>hi</u>s example, but the size, appearance and nature of the sun are a common topic in Ancient philosophy; cf Diogenes Laertius 9.85-6.

404 <u>quivering fires</u>: the whole sentence reads like an epic description of dawn – *iubar* is an Ennian word – while *tremulis ignibus* is reminiscent of Cicero's translation of Aratus' *Phaenomena* 153. Nature is personified in the way Dawn is treated in Homer, although L believes that everything operates on strict mechanical laws.

406 <u>there</u>: Bailey adopts Naugerius' *tibi* without comment for the MSS *ubi*. The correct reading is surely *ibi* (ed.Juntina) both on grounds of palaeography and sense: 'the emphatic combination *ibi tum* is appropriate in this description of a phenomenon that occurs briefly at a precise time' (M.F. Smith (Loeb edition p 308)).

406 <u>sun...mountains</u>: L juxtaposes *sol montis* as nature does so in life; cf the emphatic *fervidus igni* 407.

407-8 <u>at close quarters</u>: Bailey plausibly suggests that L is

116

setting up an antithesis here – 'the rising sun appears to touch the mountains with his sword in hand, though he is many hundred spear-throws away' (iii.p 1231).

409 five hundred...: another Ennian phrase (*Ann*.353 V³).

410-13 L expands the point to bring out the vast areas of land and sea between the sun and the mountains. Notice the expansive enjambment of 410-11, the *variatio* of *iacent...substrata...interiecta*, the assonant mirroring of sea and sky in *aequora..aetheriis* and the subtle surprise of *oris* – these shores belong to the sky, not the sea.

414-9 After the epic grandeur of the previous example, L now turns to puddles, perhaps picking up his suggestion of the sky mirrored in the sea (cf previous n). The lines have caused considerable confusion and emendation, and thus merit extended discussion. L describes the puddle in bathetically commonplace terms (414-5) to set up the paradox of such a lowly phenomenon affording a view of epic proportions (416ff). 416-7 are paralleled at Homer *Iliad* 8.16, Hesiod *Theogony* 720, Vergil *Georgics* 2.291, *Aeneid* 6.577-9, Ovid *Tristia* 1.2.19-22. In most of these examples the subject under discussion is the Underworld being as far below the earth as the sky is above it; if L is asserting that the fathomless Underworld is visible in a puddle in the street, it is at least surprising, if not absurdly exaggerated. The water will show either a reflection of the sky or the paving stones of the street. Now in the context of gazing into the Underworld 'bodies' suggests 'corpses', especially with 'hidden under the earth'; and yet we also 'seem' to see the clouds there, *below* us. L caps the whole picture of optical befuddlement with the glorious nonsense 'under the earth in the sky'. The whole point of this section of the poem is to demonstrate, partly by ridicule, the *obvious* absurdity of the so-called optical illusions which are evidence for the Sceptics' case and potentially dangerous for Epicurean epistemology. Hence the ironic exaggeration of these lines – as if anybody could fail to realise it was only an illusion, as if anybody would think that the image in the puddle ('no deeper than a finger's breadth') was of the Underworld itself complete with corpses. 'Marvellously' strikes just the right note of sarcastic astonishment. If, as Munro suggests, 'bodies' refers to 'our bodies', then that adds to the humour – the foolish man thinks he sees *himself* as a corpse in Hades. Thus the optical illusion which discredits the validity of the senses is itself discredited with scorn and humour.

418   seem: *videare videre* is emphatically juxtaposed, but leaves *videre* grammatically insecure; C.L. Howard (*Classical Philology* 56 (1961) 153-4) prints a comma after *videare*, taking *videre* and *despicere* in asyndeton – but Roman texts had no commas, and it is hard to believe that the Roman reader would not have taken *videare videre* together. (cf Townend 338). The best solution seems to be Lambinus' *videre, et*; the repeated *et..et* well suggests the open-mouthed astonishment of the foolish man.

420-5   The example of the horse stuck in the river appearing to move upstream is close to 387-90.

420   spirited..sticks: there is something of an oxymoron in the juxtaposition *acer obhaesit*.

422-3   The rhythm of these lines is appropriately jerky and uneven, as if the words themselves are struggling against the even flow of the metre. (On 422 cf West (1969) 55).

424-5   wherever we turn our eyes: notice that 'everything seems to be carried along...' only after we have gazed down into the water.

426-31   The vanishing point of the colonnade; cf Sextus Empiricus *OP* 1.118.

428   whole length: *longa* is separated from *tota* to suggest the stretching out of the colonnade; cf 429, where *angusti fastigia coni* collects all the material together into a verbal 'point'.

430   roof...floor: *tecta solo* and *dextera laevis* are again juxtaposed in words as in life.

431   point: *coni conduxit acumen* is striking for the repetition of *con-* and the assonance of *-dux-..cum-*. 'The repeated *con-* joins the four other c sounds in the line to sharpen the onomatopeia' (West (1969) 96).

432-5   Sailors who see only sea and sky 'see' the sun rising and setting from and into the sea.

432-3   rise-set: notice how *ex undis ortus* is a concentrated phrase, expressing the sudden appearance of the sun, whereas *in undis...lumen* is long drawn-out, as is the wide arc described by the sun in the course of a whole day. *ex undis ortus in undis* is of course deliberately confusing and paradoxical.

435   to stop you thinking: after 48 lines of examples, L slips

in a timely reminder of the point at issue.

436-42 The bent oar was a favourite example of illusion; cf Sextus Empiricus *OP* 1.119, Cic. *Acad.* 2.7.19, Annas and Barnes 106-9.

437-8 <u>poops..dew of the brine:</u> L's language is again epic – observe the metonymy of 'poop' and 'dew of the brine' for boat and sea-water respectively.

439 <u>upper part of the rudder:</u> notice the musical assonance of *superne guberna*, and the emphatic anaphora of *recta*.

440-2 <u>refracted...:</u> the distortion of the image is sensationalised with a string of infinitives and participles, leaving the reader in some confusion – to match the optical confusion under discussion.

443-6 Relative motion again, as at 387-90 and 420-5.

443 <u>scattered:</u> this must be the sense of *rara* – if the clouds were too solid a mass covering the sky the stars would be invisible.

447-52 Pressing the eye doubles the image; cf Sextus Empiricus *AM* 7.192; *OP* 1.47; Cic. *Acad. Prior*.2.25.80. The cause of the double image is more commonly drunkenness; cf Petronius *Sat.* 64 'By now the lamps were multiplying before my eyes'.

447 <u>hand...eye:</u> *oculo manus* recreates the movement in its verbal juxtaposition.

448 <u>presses:</u> the position of *pressit* is emphatic, suggesting a sudden hard push into the eye.

449-52 <u>double:</u> notice what West (1969) 18) calls the 'plenitude' of L's imagery; the images themselves double and redouble just as the verbal phrases multiply in a kaleidoscopic sequence.

450 <u>flowering with flame:</u> for the metaphor cf 1.900 with Brown *ad loc.* The phrase is not without scientific justification – L holds that trees and other combustible things contain within them the 'seeds of fire'. Notice the musical effect of *luc- flor- lum- fla-*.

452 <u>men with two faces...:</u> again L deliberately makes the illusion as ridiculous as possible, recalling here perhaps Aristophanes' speech in Plato's *Symposium* 189c2-d6.

453-61 Dreams are obviously illusions, and form a suitable conclusion to this section. (They are further discussed later in the book at 962-1036.)

453 <u>fettered:</u> cf 1027, Ennius *Ann* 5 V^3. Notice the hushed s alliteration of 453-4, transformed into hard c alliteration at 456-8 when L describes the dreams themselves.

456-7 <u>blind...see:</u> L again engineers paradox in the antithesis of *caeca/cernere*. Notice also the asyndeton of 458, pointing to the absurd quantity of natural landscape which we exchange for our 'confined space'.

461 <u>words...silent:</u> paradox again.

462-8 L concludes his catalogue with a restatement of his position (cf 379-86) that in all these cases it is the judgement of the mind, not the senses themselves, which are responsible.

462 <u>undermine:</u> *violare...quaerunt* is a bold personification, apologised for in 'as it were'.

465 <u>mental preconceptions:</u> Epicurus' *to prosdoxazomenon* (cf Bailey 253-7) amounts to Cicero's word *opinio* for jumping to conclusions on the basis of inadequate evidence; the Sceptic of course will assert that no amount of data is ever sufficient to determine the truth of a theory.

468 <u>readily:</u> *protinus* suggests precisely the premature certainty which L is condemning.

469 - 521 SCEPTICISM

This passage is in many ways the philosophical heart of the book, the objective of which is to demonstrate that - and how - the perceptions of our senses are to be trusted. L has gone through the many cases of sense-experience deceiving us, only to show now that, for all the superficial plausibility of the sceptic's case, his position is philosophically untenable. He first argues *a priori* that the proposition 'I know that I know nothing' is analytically self-refuting, with the stock reasoning that knowledge of one's own ignorance is none the less knowledge. He then argues at greater length *a posteriori* that even a weak form of this scepticism ('I *only* know that I know nothing' - reminiscent of Socrates' famous 'irony' cf Plato *Apology* 23 ab) is likewise incoherent, as the very notion of knowledge (presupposed in the notion of ignorance) comes from sense-experience, which we are only able to evaluate as reliable or unreliable insofar as we can distinguish degrees of veracity; in practical terms, we only recognise delusions as such because the rest of the time we are not deluded - and in any case our very survival depends on our trusting the sense-datum which informs us when we are about to walk over a cliff. This does not, of course, dispose of the sceptic entirely. Thorough-going scepticism refuses to accept the validity of any belief - even the belief in ignorance - on the grounds that all beliefs will turn out groundless if pushed hard enough – leaving a despair about knowledge whose permanent response to any question is a shrug of the shoulders. If L's ridicule of the practical consequences of scepticism seems exaggerated, they are not; ancient sceptics seem to have practised their scepticism in everyday life, ignoring danger as possibly hallucination and only being saved by less sceptical friends (see 509-10n).

Sceptical philosophy is deeply rooted in Greek thought, from the theological scepticism of Xenophanes (see Kirk, Raven and Schofield 179-80), through the provocative ideas of the Sophists (e.g. Gorgias' treatise *On nature and the non-existent* where he declares: 'Being does not exist; if it did we could not know it, if we knew it we could not communicate it'; on which see Kerferd 93-100) to the fully-developed scepticism of Pyrrho – a philosopher whose objective of serenity (*ataraxia*) is close to that of Epicurus himself, but whose philosophy of empirical non-commitment was far removed from Epicurus' epistemology. (On the relationship of Epicurus to Pyrrho see Sedley (1976)136-7, and Barigazzi 290-1). In the atomist tradition also scepticism was rife: Democritus asserted that 'in reality we know nothing' (frag.117, Kirk, Raven and Schofield 410-11), Epicurus' teacher Nausiphanes was 'an atomist with sceptical inclinations' (Rist 4: cf Diogenes Laertius 9.64 for the evidence). The Academy of Plato was 'converted' to scepticism when Arcesilaus of Pitane became its head, and remained sceptical for the next two centuries – and just as the influence began to wane (in the Academy, at least) there emerged the figure of Aenesidemus, who probably originated the famous Ten Modes of Scepticism, in many ways the definitive statement of ancient scepticism. (See Annas and Barnes, passim). Thus scepticism was no slight opponent to face: it informed a good deal of the thinking of many of the famous names in presocratic philosophy (cf Barnes 136-51), it underlay much of the relativistic speculation of the Sophistic movement, it even formed a deviationist school within Atomism (deviationist, that is, to Epicurus); and it was still very much a living force in philosophy in L's lifetime.

469-70   L's argument is as follows:
          1) No proposition can be known as true
          2) 1) is a proposition in itself
        ∴3) (1) is self-refuting.
The logic is of course unconvincing. Our despair at

121

knowing anything at all about the world may well extend to doubting our own doubts, without any inconsistency; L appears to be tilting rather at the Socratic position of only knowing one thing, viz that we know nothing. The Sceptic does not even assert his uncertainty but shrugs his shoulders on both sides of every contradiction.

472 All editors (except Merrill and Martin) follow Lachmann in emending *suo* to *sua*. Dalzell ((1960) 99) justifies the emendation by pointing out that there are no instances in L and few in Classical Latin where *in* is separated from both adjective and substantive except by an enclitic. M.F. Burnyeat (197-206) has argued convincingly that L's phrase is a poetic translation of Epicurus' *perikato trepesthai*, 'to turn around and upside down', used by him to charge the Sceptic with self-refutation; certainly L's grotesque picture of the acrobatic contortion is a brilliant piece of polemic writing.

474-7 concept: 'A characteristic Epicurean argument' (Bailey). The point is simply that a man who was genuinely ignorant would not know he was ignorant as he would not have the concept of ignorance available to him; still less would he be able to handle ideas such as 'doubtful' and 'certain'. For the argument from *notities* (concepts) cf 5.181-6, 1046-9, Cic. *De Natura Deorum* 1.16.43 - 17.45, Bailey 419-21, 439-41.

480-5 For something...: L hammers his points home with emphatic repetition of key words and phrases: *nam maiore fide debet... quid maiore fide... debet; ab sensu orta... ab sensibus orta*. The juxtaposition of *sensu falso ratio* (483) is itself expressive of the inextricable dependence of *ratio* upon *sensus* - *sensu falso* entails *falsa ratio*, as is asserted in 485.

486-8 ears..eyes...: L presents a cartoon picture of the war of the senses to ridicule the idea, linking the various senses in neat chiastic pairs: *oculos aures.. aures tactus.. tactum sapor*, ending the sequence, as it began, with the eyes. L strives to vary the verbs - they all connote 'refute' but there is a sequence of censure (*reprehendere*), formal accusation (*arguet*), stun into silence (*confutabunt*) and finally win the case (*revincent*). Notice how it is the mouth which is credited with the verbal fireworks in *arguet*, and notice how variation is achieved in the four 'an..' questions by different lengths of phrases, the last one being a rounded whole line.

489-96 capability peculiar to itself: L argues that the senses cannot refute one another, since their modes of perception are different (but cf 230-8n). In fact where the evidence of the senses conflicts it is usually sight which 'wins', at least over touch; cf Annas and Barnes 69-73.

493 whatever things are joined up with the colours: by this L surely means shape - the twin properties of images are shape and colour (cf e.g. 243).

497-8 not..criticise themselves: the tower looks square when near, round when far, but there is no reason to decide which (if either) of the two 'views' is correct. This is the kernel of the Sceptics' case; if we receive contradictory perceptions of the same thing with the same sense, how can we know which is right? a fortiori, how can we decide between senses? If any are wrong, then they may all be wrong. Epicurus takes the opposite, sanguine view that: 1) perception is caused by images, which must be material to affect matter, ∴2) all perception is perception of something. If we decide that that horse is a cow, that is our fault, not the horse's. Therefore 3) all perceptions are true (499) (cf Taylor).

500-510 Even if we cannot explain why our senses are at odds with each other (and themselves) it is better to persevere with them rather than give up all trust, which would both destroy the basis of all reasoning and endanger life itself.

501 were...look: it might be argued that L has pre-empted the conclusion in his choice of verbs, declaring that the towers are square in a way the Sceptic would refuse to acknowledge.

502-3 untruthfully: the ethical and practical salvation offered by Epicurus transcends the search for total explanations.

504 graspable...grasp: manibus manifesta is an obvious 'jingle...to stress the obviousness of what we have lost' (West (1969) 96; cf Snyder 99-100).

505 most basic: cf 1.423, 693-5 for the primacy of faith in the senses.

505-7 collapse...fall..: L applies metaphors from the collapse of buildings (fundamenta...ruat..concidat), picked up and developed at 513-21.

508 courage: ironical tone here - you need courage to avoid walking over a cliff.

509-10 precipitous places: cf Diogenes Laertius' *Life of Pyrrho* (9.62), where it is reported that this famous Sceptic 'faced all risks..traffic, precipices, dogs...', being kept out of harm's way by his faithful friends.

513-21 building: L seems to be taking his comparison from the play of words whereby in Greek *kanon* is both a mason's ruler and the title of a work by Epicurus (D.L. 10.31). For the comparison cf also Plato *Laws* 793c, West (1969) 69-72.

517 crooked...: the contradictory catalogue of instability in breathless asyndeton well expresses the house tumbling down on all sides. (cf a similar phrase at Homer *Iliad* 23.116).

518-9 fall down: L now picks up 507-8; 'The parts which wish to fall immediately (*iam ruere*) clearly correspond to life itself (*concidat extemplo*); the whole building (*ruantque omnia*) refers to the whole of their reasoning (*ruantque omnia*)..' (West (1969) 71).

521 false: as Bailey astutely notes, the word must be understood in inverted commas.

522 other senses: hearing (524-614) taste (615-72) and smell (673-721). L does not deal separately with touch (cf 265-8n).

524-7 L's argument is circular; *corpore* (525) 'proves' that sound is *corpoream*, just as *pepulere* is picked up by *impellere*.

528-41 L attempts to prove the corporeal nature of voice with examples of the physical effects of the volume and duration of speech.

528-34 crowd: L describes the shouting voice as being like a crowd in a passage (*fauces* is often used of an architectural passage, see *OLD* s.v.3d). Notice the harsh v, f and c sounds.

529 windpipe rougher: a reference to the Greek term for the windpipe *tracheia arteria* (*trachus* = rough = *asper*).

532 congested: the sense of the line is fairly clear – the voice particles come out in greater numbers than usual and form a bottleneck when they reach the doorway from the throat ·to the mouth and scrape it. *expletis* must agree with *faucibus* (528); although it is the *ianua oris* which is scraped, this only happens when the throat is congested.

534 injure: 'I hurt, therefore I am' principle; cf 2.436.

537-8 rising gleam of dawn...: L may be mocking the

grandiloquent orators who would filibuster bills in the Senate by talking them out, as Leonard and Smith suggest. Certainly this would make the inflated style of these lines more pointed.

542-8 Differences of sound-quality must stem from differences in the sound-particles themselves, so that smooth atoms make smooth sounds, etc. (cf 622-6, where the same principle explains different tastes). The identity of the sound as located in the atomic constitution is underlined by the repetition *asperitas...asperitate* (542).

546 boxwood...: this line and the next are incurably corrupt, yet the sense is relatively clear; we have a two-way contrast of brass instruments and high-pitched birdsong (or a three-way contrast if Giussani is right to see in 546 a different sound from either 545 or 547 concealed under the corrupt *retro cita*). Giussani printed Vossius' *Berecyntia* (sc.*tibia*) for *retro cita*, comparing Catullus 64.263-4; but Catullus is contrasting the bass *bombos* with the treble *stridebat tibia*. If L were similarly comparing bass reed with treble reed with treble voice (a double contrast of pitch and timbre) this would be effective: but *bombum* in 546 makes it clear that the instrument concealed behind *retro cita* is low in pitch, and trumpet-like in tone (*raucus*). The best solution is Büchner's *buxus cita*, the boxwood pipe closely associated with the cult of Cybele (Claudian *de rapt. Pros.* 1.211, V.*Aen.*9.619, Statius *Theb.*2.77. Ovid *Met.* 4.30) and so with the right Eastern credentials to support *barbara*. The sound is also *raucus* ('*pectora rauco concita buxo* Seneca *Ag.* 689) and deep ('*inflati murmure buxi* Ovid *Met.*14.537, corresponding to *murmur* in 545 here - cf *mugit* Statius *Theb.*9.479 = *mugit* 545). Richter (66f) objects to *buxus* because 1) it is too high to emit *bombos* (but see the passages quoted above, ignored by Richter) 2) anyway *citus* is not used of instruments, only voices (but cf Cat.64.262, V.*Geor.*4.64). It is at least worth arguing that *citus* might mean 'swift' in this case - i.e. capable of rapid playing; cf Cic. *de Orat.* 3.216 on *cita* and *tarda* sounds from an instrument, or Cat.63.74 *sonitus citus* - almost certainly the *buxus* was more virtuoso than the *tuba*.

547 icy chill...: the MSS reading is again corrupt. Argument has focussed on the nature of the bird in question; thus we have had the swan - although swans singing are not a

125

common occurrence, especially on the slopes of Mt Helicon, – and anyway the swan song is only infrequently a lament (the swan at Eur. *Electra* 151 is given something to weep over) – and the nightingale, a more promising candidate to typify the lamenting bird (cf Homer *Odyssey* 19.518ff, quoted by Richter). Then we still have the problem of Helicon – how often does the Roman reader have the sensation of hearing a nightingale on Mt Helicon? When L relies so much on everyday life for his examples it is hard to imagine him indulging this precious allusion, unless he has a literary point to make – and none of the commentators have so far shown that he has.

It is therefore preferable to take the line right out of the mythological world with Richter's suggestion (adopted in the text), which turns the following line from an allusion to a generalisation. The association of bird-song and night-time suggests the nightingale, which is then amplified in *lugubri voce querallam*. What matters to the argument is the timbre of bird-song, not ornithological or mythological sophistication; if the reader picks up the reference to the nightingale, well and good; if he does not, the phrase still recreates the sound-qualities which are the central point at issue.

549-94   L now turns from sound to speech; the origins of language are discussed at 5.1028-62. Words are clearly of enormous interest to L, and there is a nice consistency in the theory of images and the use of language – words, like images, are not the things they represent, but they communicate those things, and indeed the mere mention of the word is sufficient to cause the images of the thing to appear in the mind (785).

551   saws them into sections: the tongue is like a carpenter, taking the mass of raw material and dividing it up into meaningful shapes of different sizes and sounds.

553   race: *spatium* is a metaphor from racing – cf 1196. Notice how sound travels more slowly than visual images; cf 6.164ff on the obvious example of thunder and lightning.

555-6   joint by joint...: *articulatim* picks up *articulat* (551), 556 picks up 552. The repetition is not just catechism-like incantation; it also evinces the faithful transmission of sound from source (549-52) to receiver (554-6).

558   distorted: words are like images in this respect; cf L's explanation of the square tower images at 357-9.

560 feel the sound: not synaesthesia - merely a reminder that sounds are heard by their contact with the body.

562 encumbered: note the expressive tmesis of *inque pedita* - the sound is broken up just like the compound participle.

563ff crier: the word *praeco* here means the official at the law courts and other formal public proceedings (*OLD* s.v. 1b); *in populo* suggests 'in the public assembly'.

565 voice...voices: note the polyptoton *voces vox* to bring out the multiplicity of voices arising out of a single voice.

567 stamping a shape: i.e. imprinting like a wax seal and a signet-ring (cf 2.581). Notice the dichotomy between the 'shape' and the 'sound'; the shape of the word will determine how it is understood, irrespective of the volume of noise emitted - but the crier must see that *his* sound is 'clear'.

568 fall into: *incidit* suggests the random, spray-gun scattering of sound by the crier to all and sundry - it is a matter of chance whether the sound falls into the ears.

569 idly...breezes: for the common idea of futility expressed thus cf 1096, Otto s.v. *ventus* 2.

570-9 Echoes. If any atoms can bounce, then they all can; cf 150-1, 269-323 on mirrors. In this section *imagine* (571) is a visual term more appropriate to mirrors than echoes, used here to underline the consistency of the mechanics in both cases.

571 deluding: L may be thinking of Aristophanes' *Thesmophoriazusae* 1059-97 where Echo is called *epikokkastria* (mocker) and teases the Scythian Archer mercilessly; or perhaps the pathetic myths of Eurydice (cf V *Geor.*4.525-7 where the river-banks re-echo the name uttered by the decapitated Orpheus) or Hylas (V. *Ecl.*6.44 - which fits 575ff rather well).

574 the exact shapes of words: just like the mask dashed against the pillar (296-301), except that the correct sequence of words is maintained.

575-6 straying companions: cf 5.974. As often, L locates his scientific theory in a landscape charged with emotion.

577 seen: cf 598n.

578 hills...hills: echoing polyptoton.

579 trained: MSS *dicta* is otiose with *verba*, whereas Lachmann's *docta* adds a superb touch of humour - the words are like dogs trained to come back to their master.

580-94 L indulges in a short satire on the myths of country folk; for comparable material cf Herodotus 6.105, Pindar

Pythian 3.79, Pausanias 9.25.3, Homer *Iliad* 24.614-6 Dodds 117 +n.87, West ad Hesiod *Theogony* 22-35.

580 <u>goat-footed Satyrs</u>: these were attendants of Dionysus and spirits of woods and hills; they were grotesque, partly bestial (*semiferi* 587) and insatiably randy. Plutarch records the tale that the Roman general Sulla caught a satyr and brought him back to Italy in 83 BC (Plutarch *Sulla* 27) – so perhaps L is not tilting at windmills in this little tirade.

581 <u>fauns</u>: these were Italian nature-spirits, equivalent to the satyrs and identified with them.

582 <u>playful pranks</u>: satyrs are linked with comedy – cf the Greek tradition of the Satyr play (on which see now Euripides' *Cyclops* ed. Seaford pp 1-5), and yet they are also a repository of wisdom (cf V.*Ecl*.6).

583 <u>speechless silences</u>: not merely a tautology – the awful natural silence of the night cows the peasant into speechlessness.

584-5 <u>pipe</u>: the pan-pipes spring to mind, the seven-pipe syrinx named after the nymph who was turned into a reed to escape Pan (cf Ovid *Met*.1.689-712), but the reference to it being 'struck by the players' fingers' shows that this is the single reed with stops; the pan-pipes *are* mentioned in 588. For this single *tibia* cf 5.1384, V.*Ecl*.2.36. The apparent paradox of 'sweet sad' recalls a long tradition in Greek literature of the pleasure evoked by the artistic representation of pain – see C.W. Macleod's edition of Homer *Iliad* 24, p.7 n.4.

587 <u>pine</u>: the pine was sacred to Pan. Notice the chiastic order of *pinea¹ semiferi² capitis² velamina¹*.

588-9 L very much enters the atmosphere of pastoral poetry here – doubtless with ironic intent – in a way which influenced Vergil (cf Coleman ad *Ecl*.1.2). The bathos of the passage lies in the next five cynical lines, undercutting the pastoral pose so adroitly built up – cf Horace *Epode* 2 for precisely the same effect.

594 <u>little ears</u>: *auricularum* is the MSS reading and makes excellent sense as a genitive similar to *ferox animi* (Ernout); i.e. their ears (rendered comic by the patronising diminutive) are greedy for the kind of silly stories he has just told us. This is preferable to Bailey's 'over-eager to catch the ears', as the supply of people boasting of these tales must be matched by a corresponding demand to hear them.

595-614 Sound particles travel through barriers impermeable to visual images, and they also fly in all directions from the emitting body.

598 <u>aware:</u> *conloquium..videmus* has excited remark; yet parallels such as *V.Aen.*4.490, Prop.2.16.49 (cf *OLD* s.v. *video* 9b) make it clear that the verb can connote perception in general and not merely sight in particular. It is particularly surprising that none of the commentators have noticed the explicit remark of Quintilian 10.1.13 'For both "I understand" (*intellego*) and "I feel" (*sentio*) and "I see" (*video*) often have the same force as "I know" (*scio*)'.

599-600 <u>images refuse:</u> the brusque refusal of the images in two words is deliberately abrupt after the sinuous eight words describing the flexible voice.

604-6 <u>sounds..sounds:</u> the instant generation of sounds from a single sound is brought out by the polyptoton *aliis aliae; gignuntur* leads on to the parallel of *ignis* in paronomasia as at 330-1, and 606 is the most prolonged alliteration in the poem, suggesting the sparks spitting out of the fire.

607-8 <u>well away from sight:</u> the point at issue here is the contrast between visual images, which are only perceived when in the direct line of fire, and auditory images which can move backwards, round corners and through walls. *fervunt* is Munro's emendation for the MSS corrupt *fuerunt*.

611 <u>hedge:</u> the MSS *saepe* (hedge) has been emended by many editors needlessly. Although *saepe* in this neuter form is not recorded elsewhere, *praesepe* is reasonably common. Lachmann's *intra* is quite unnecessary – the situation visualised is presumably that of a man trying to look over a wall or hedge into (say) a garden; even though he cannot see over, he can still hear sounds although he remains outside (in the street).

612-4 <u>yet...:</u> a qualification to L's breezy confidence about the ability of voices to pass 'unscathed' through barriers (599-600).

615-32 The mechanics of taste.

615-6 <u>Nor:</u> *nec* (Marullus) is certainly right; Epicurean epistemology rests on the principle that sensation arises through physical contact beteen subject and object. On this reasoning, taste is obviously easier to explain than hearing. The MSS *plus opere* needs emendation:

Lachmann's *plus operaeve* has a needlessly deferred *-ve*, Martin's *plus operai* has to be taken in asyndeton with the previous line. As a compromise I have printed *plusve operai* which restores the sense without either difficulty.

615-7 <u>feel taste</u>: the repetition *sentimus sucum...sucum sentimus* is partly to stress the operative word *sentimus* running through all the accounts of the different senses, partly as an incantatory question-and-answer form.

620-1 <u>spread out</u>: the winding path of the juice as it is absorbed is conveyed in the sandwiching of words; *quod'...caulas² omne' palati²... rarae³..flexa⁴ foramina⁴ linguae³*.

623-4 <u>sweetly</u>: L attempts to convey the pleasure of the taste with the anaphora of *suaviter*, the enjambment stressing *umida* which is then intensified by *sudantia* and the elevated term *templa* (cf 5.103).

625-6 <u>on the other hand</u>: the contrast in style is marked, from the elevated to the nasty; notice the effective contrast in verbs – *attingunt:pungunt, tractant:lacerant*. The phrase 'filled with roughness' is interesting – *repletus* is often used of a glutton sated with food (*OLD* s.v. *repleo* 5), setting up a nice irony in which the food itself is 'stuffed'.

628 <u>plunged</u>: the expressive verb *praecipitavit* inclines *fauces* towards its common metaphorical sense of 'the entrance to a cave..esp. of the Underworld' (*OLD* s.v.3e); cf 1.724, 6.639.

630-2 <u>Nor does it matter at all</u>: L merely means that simple food is no less pleasurable than luxurious food, since once pain (hunger) has been assuaged the pleasure cannot be increased, only varied (Epicurus *Men* 130-1). For a similar argument applied to clothing cf 5.1423-33.

632 <u>sturdy condition</u>: the MSS read *umidum*, emended by Bailey and Munro to Lachmann's *umidulum*, without explaining why L should at this point appear to insist on digestive juices. L's argument is that 1) we only enjoy food while it is in the mouth; 2) anything digestible may be eaten. Orth (*Helmantica* 11 (1960) 318) reads *validum*, quoting Q. Serenus Sammonicus' *Liber Medicinalis* 302 'a sturdy condition (*validus tenor*) of this (the stomach) strengthens all the limbs'. While not ideal – the parallel passage is very late – this does fit better with the theme of primitiveness adumbrated in 630.

633 <u>for us to see</u>: there is no reason to emend the MSS *ut*

videamus which is abundantly clear; Bailey's emendation *atque venenum* anticipates the effective contrast in 637 and thereby weakens it, Lachmann's *unicus aptus* is nonsense after L's point that we can eat anything we like.

635 The infinitive *esse* could come from either *edo* (I eat) or *sum* (I am). The latter is clearly correct, but the former is not inappropriate in this section.

638-9 snake: there is a nice irony in the suggestion that the snake is poisoned by saliva, as saliva is credited with healing properties, especially against snake-poison (cf Pliny *N.H.* 28,35; 7,13:15); thus what man has in his mouth poisons snakes, what snakes have in their mouths poisons men. Bailey and other editors believe that *est itaque* conceals the name of a snake, e.g. *excetra* (Ellis), *skytale* (Bailey); and yet Pliny seems to assert that it is all men and all snakes so affected, not just one species (*NH* 7.2.15). This does, however, cast doubt on *est* — not 'there is a snake' but simply 'snakes...' would seem to be required. Richter's *pestifera ut* is brilliant, but palaeographically difficult, adding to the ironic tone the twist that the poisoner is itself poisoned.

638ff L here has to deal with another pillar of the Sceptic's case, viz the disparity between 1) human taste and animal taste and 2) disparities between individuals' responses to common foods or poisons. On all this see Annas and Barnes 31-65.

640-1 Hellebore...fat: the same paradox, only applied to hemlock, appears at Sextus Empiricus *OP* 1.57, D.L. 9.80, Galen *On Temperaments* IV 684K; cf also *DRN* 5.899-900.

643-51 The obvious external differences in shape must extend also to internal differences of atomic constitution. Sextus Empiricus *OP* 1.52-4 explains the variation in taste in exactly the same way, drawing the comparison with the effects of fever in men just as L does at 664ff.

647 external contour: *circumcaesura* corresponds to Epicurus' *perikope*. It only occurs here and at 3.219.

648 differing shape: Lachmann's *variante figura* is needed to make the line significant; to leave the MSS reading *variantque figura* would leave the first half of the line expressing merely the jejune statement that they are composed of atoms, when the essential point is that their atoms differ in shape.

649 different: *distent, differre* picks up *distantia differitasque* (636).

650 gaps..passages...channels: L searches through the available words to convey his meaning.

652-4 Notice the anaphora of *esse...esse*, the chiasmus of *triquetra aliis aliis quadrata*, the *variatio* of *debent... necessest;* furthermore the multiplicity of variations is well evinced by *multa... multis multangula*, where *multa* is logically unnecessary in company with *quaedam* in 654.

655-7 The three determinants of the shape of the channels are: 1) the arrangement of the shapes of the constituent atoms, 2) the movement of the atoms (see 2.308-32 on the constant motion of the atoms) and 3) the atomic texture.

658 pleasant...bitter: note chiasmus of *suave est aliis /aliis fit amarum*.

660-1 caressingly: *contractabiliter* only occurs here; for its sensuous connotations see *OLD* s.v. *contrecto* 2. Notice how the four long words of 460 suggest the languorous pleasure, the shorter words of 461 the stabbing bitterness.

662 throat: there is some apparent inconsistency here with 627 — unless L is using the word metaphorically of the channels themselves.

664 bile gets the upper hand: the phrase ought to refer to jaundice — but cf also the comparable passage in Sextus Empiricus *OP* 1.52 'when in fevers.. we are affected.. depending on the different dominance in us of the so-called humours'. (Bile was one of the four humours).

668 it then happens...: the word order of the line is as confused as the atoms.

671 honey: for the sensory ambivalence of honey cf Sextus Empiricus *OP* 1.92, Seneca *Ep*. 109.7.

672 in the past: cf 2.398-407; 3.191-5.

673 - 705 SMELL

L's account is very brief, since the principle has already been explained in the accounts of other senses; a smell travels like a sound and affects us like a taste — smells come from deep down (695) as do tastes (618) and only trigger the sensation when atomically suited to do so. Thus although smells are objective, the response varies widely in view of the wide variations in atomic structure. See Epicurus *Hdt* 53, Bailey 242, 354, 404-6.

675-6 flowing stream...flowing: 'A good instance of L's indifference to repetition' (Bailey). Far from being indifferent, the repetition is contrived to convey the unbroken stream of odours of all kinds. For *volvat* used of smells cf 6.1154.

676 flowing..discharged..spread: a triad of infinitives progressing from the gentle *fluere* to the directed *mitti* to the more violent *spargi*.

677-8 differing shapes: perception of smell depends on the atoms of the smell fitting the channels of the body like a jigsaw puzzle.

678-80 through the breezes: bees and vultures are extreme examples of the divergent power of smells, but are both flying things, to bring out the sense of 'however far away...'. Again L seems to be drawing on the examples furnished by the Sceptics; cf Sextus Empiricus *OP* 1.55-6.

680-3 force of hounds: these lines are reminiscent of earlier Latin poetry, with the strong f and ss alliteration, the epic periphrasis *canum vis* (cf e.g. Homer *Iliad* 23.720, V.*Aen*.4.132) culminating in the patriotic tale of the goose saving Rome from the Gauls in 387 BC (see Livy 5.47.1-4) alluded to with the grandiose *Romulidarum arcis servator*. There is nothing surprising in L indulging patriotic sensibilities in his Roman audience and at the same time demonstrating his technical powers.

684-6 shy away from foul poison: L exaggerates the degree to which smell saves us from poisoning ourselves; cf 5.1009, where early man often poisoned himself unwittingly. Notice the effective collocation of *taetro resilire veneno*; the violence of the response (*resilire*) is enclosed by the foul stimulus.

687-705 Smells are less mobile than sounds and sights, since they come from deep down inside bodies and furthermore they are made up of grosser particles.

690-1 as..as..not to mention: the anaphora of *quam* builds up a nice tricolon crescendo figure, the third element in the sequence being lengthened by the *recusatio* figure ('not to mention...').

692 lose its way: the smell is like a bad messenger who gets lost and arrives late; cf 703-5.

693 breezes: symbol of futility again – cf 569n, 1096.

694 with difficulty: Bailey notes that the double *ex* and *vix*, with the consequent halting rhythm of the line, may suggest the difficulty of emission of the smell.

695 <u>flow</u>: notice the musical assonance of <u>recedere</u> <u>rebus</u> <u>odores</u>, suggesting the easy flow of the smells.

696-7 <u>broken, crushed...</u>: notice the triple anaphora of *quod*.

699-700 <u>does not penetrate</u>: contradicted later (6.951-2).

703-4 <u>cold..dilatory</u>: the impact of the smell is described in metaphorical terms appropriate to a messenger running with a letter. While he runs hard he is hot (*calida*), but if he dawdles (*cunctando*) he gets cold (*refrigescit*). The natural way to read *nuntia* is thus as fem. sing. with *plaga*, not as neuter plural substantive; and this requires the emendation of MSS *decurrunt* to Lambinus' *decurrit* (M.F. Smith points out that the *-unt* corruption may have come from *nuntia*).

706-21 L neatly effects a return to the notion of images, to prepare the way for the discussion of thought, without any harsh dislocation of thought-sequence; the fact that different species have different tastes in sight no less than in food and smell continues L's theme of the possibility of (apparently) subjective variations in perception. The material again is drawn from the Sceptics, who have many more examples of the same phenomenon to quote (see Sextus Empiricus *OP* 1.58).

710 <u>applaud</u>: *explaudere* is a metaphor from the theatre, meaning literally 'to drive an actor offstage'.

711 <u>dawn</u>: notice the placing of *clara* immediately after *auroram* for effect and the clucking repetition of sound (c) and word-root (*voce vocare*).

712 <u>impossible to stand up to</u>: Sextus Empiricus (*OP* 1.58) also quotes the inability of elephants to face rams, sea-beasts to hear the crackling of pounded beans, and tigers to hear drums.
<u>ravening</u>: *rabidi* (Wakefield) is surely correct for the MSS *rapidi* - cf 5.892 for the same corruption. *rapidi* has been justified as meaning *rapaces* (*OLD* s.v. *rapidus* 4) but the contrast between the cock and the lion is better drawn with the berserk *rabidi*.

717 <u>for all their ferocity</u>: *feroces* has concessive force.

719-21 <u>hurting</u>: as Bailey remarks, L appears to have forgotten his earlier theory of the images, whereby all images are made up of superfine particles, in asserting here that some particles cannot penetrate the eyes. L has already mentioned the possibility of sight being painful to the eyes at 324-31.

Having established the tactile nature of sense-perception, L now proceeds to prove the tactile nature of thought. If everything is made up of physical atoms, then the mind is also material (proved in book 3); only matter can affect matter, which proves that thoughts and dreams are also material – thought therefore is sensation, *phronesis* is *aisthesis*.

L explains the mechanics of thought in terms of images, such that thought-images are like sight-images, only finer still, able to enter the mind through the pores of the body and thus pass directly into the mental bloodstream (730-1). The implication of this is that our thought-process is essentially passive, the only freedom being the selection of which of the available images to concentrate on – and L has to argue then (794ff) that the variety of available images present to the mind is colossal. Abstract ideas are hard to explain on this theory – in particular the concept of the void (*inane*) as opposed to matter (*res*); L has dilated at length on the subject of the void (1.329-97), thus demonstrating that we can think about it, and yet it would be nonsense to assert that there could be an 'image' of 'nothing' which stimulates thought/sensation.

725 everywhere..great: L stresses the abundance of images with the collocation of *multa..multis...cunctas undique*.
727 spider's web: the analogy is consistent with 3.381-90, where L demonstrated that some things are too fine to be felt by the body; similarly here L is about to argue that mental images are too fine to be perceived by the relatively gross eye-atoms. (728-31).
729-31 take over...stimulate: the passivity of both sensation and thought is brought out by the power ascribed to the images themselves.
732-43 L is again on his hobby-horse of the Centaur (cf 129-42; 5.878-924; 2.700-17) and other grotesque monsters, and he again refers to the visions of the dead (cf 26-44n); this both suits his personal crusade against superstition and his scientific wonder at the marvels of perception.
732-3 Centaurs..Scyllas...Cerberean: the Centaur was a monster with the head and torso of a man on the body of a horse. Scylla was a sea-monster with twelve feet and six heads. Cerberus was the three-headed guard dog of

the Underworld – which leads L nicely into the topic of ghosts.

Notice in these lines how 'limbs' and 'faces' rather load the argument – by this anatomical dissection he prepares the reader for the theory of composite images.

734 **bones the earth embraces:** the phrase reminds one of the language of epitaphs (cf also 761).

740 **animal:** The MSS reading *anima* is clearly corrupt. Of the two emendations worth considering, *animalis* makes better sense than *animantis; animans* connotes all living creatures, including man, whereas *animal* expresses the right sort of distance between man and 'beast' appropriate in discussing a non-existent mutation such as the Centaur (see *OLD* s.v. *animal* for its generally pejorative sense).

741 **horse and..man:** the slapping together of incongruous images is well brought out by the jerky rhythm and harsh elisions of this line.

745–8 **any single one:** unlike sight, which depends on a coherent stream of images, thought can be aroused by a single image. This idea – which is unparalleled in other Epicurean texts – doubtless helps to explain how such a colossal repertoire of thought-provoking images is constantly available to us.

750–1 **like...like:** the repetition of *simili* reinforces the uniform nature of all images, and plays on the word *simulacrum* (image).

755 **images of lions:** *per simulacra leonum* (OQ) is the correct reading; Lachmann's *leonem* (to fit *cetera*) only makes the construction difficult, and *cetera* is merely short for *ceterorum quae*.

757–76 **sleep:** the phenomenon of sleep helps to prove L's assertion that the images do not enter through the senses but through the pores of the body direct into the mind, since we 'see' dreams when our eyes are shut. L further draws on the inconsequentiality of dreams to support his theory that all manner of images enter the mind, the difference being that the sleeper has no conscious powers of discrimination between sense and nonsense. Cf 5.62–3, 3.112–16, Bailey 414–5.

758 **intellect of the mind:** this is qualified at 765 by the assertion that the memory is dormant.

758–9 **awake...awake:** the repetition *vigilat..vigilamus* underlines the point of the perpetual susceptibility of the mind to the perception of images.

136

760   <u>seem to see a man...</u>: there seems no good reason why we should not in that case also 'see' the dead in waking life: L does not explain the comparative rarity of this except by hinting that our critical faculties dismiss such images, perhaps before we have even become conscious of them. Notice also the irony of 'quite clearly' of a perception which is most unreliable.

766   <u>answer back</u>: *dissentit* also contains the vital root *sentit* (feeling).

768-76   Asmis has pointed out that this passage is out of place here, consisting as it does of the answer to a question which is not posed until 788-93; she proposes transposing them to 815*816. This would tighten up the logical sequence of this part of the poem, but there is no parallel for as many as nine verses transposed by as many as 36 lines – and besides, L often floats his arguments around for rhetorical purposes, pre-empting questions before they arise and leaving the reader with conclusions already 'fixed'. L may also still be concerned with the question of the single-image thought – how can one image alone give the effect of movement? The answer is given (771) that moving dream figures do need more than one image.

769   <u>in rhythm</u>: *in numerum* probably has the sense of an ordered sequence of movements.

771-2   <u>different position</u>: the process is exactly that of cartoon animation.

774-5   <u>such...so great...</u>: note the tricolon of *tanta...tanta, tanta*, the first two being stressed at opposite ends of the line.

777-87   If anything can be subjective, then surely thought must be – and yet L has proposed a theory of mental activity such that all thought is perception of invading images over which our only control is acceptance or rejection. He now tackles the hard question of how we are able to visualise at will anything we want, however far removed from our surroundings. The answer (794-822) is to reassert that thought is essentially the mind's eye focussing on selected images, a vast range of which are permanently available. Thus subjectivity is relegated to the (unexplained) appetitive force of pleasure (*libido*) which selects the desired images.

777   <u>Many</u>: L only in fact tackles two.

779   <u>desire</u>: see 777-87n.

781-3 **keep guard:** L sarcastically sets up a ludicrous alternative explanation, endowing the images with senses of their own and personifying them as our servants, in order to make his real explanation comparatively sensible.

783 **sea, land or sky:** notice the effective tricolon crescendo: 1) *si mare* 2) *si terram cordist* 3) *si denique caelum*, the build-up heightened by the anaphora of *si*.

784 **assemblies, procession...:** the inexhaustible range of images is conveyed by the breathless asyndeton.

785 **to order:** *sub verbo* may also, as Giussani suggests, refer to the link between language and thought.

786-7 The members of a crowd can all be thinking of different things – and conversely, people miles apart may imagine the same thing.

788-93 L returns to the question (already answered 768-76) of moving dream images, to draw both questions together under a single answer (794ff) with repetitions of points already made (e.g. 800-1 = 771-2) for pedagogical, not to say disingenuous, purposes (cf Classen, 82-4).

788-91 **stirring..supple limbs:** the epanalepsis of *mollia...mollia* exactly suggests the dreamy *perpetuum mobile* L wishes to evoke in 'repeating the position'. We seem to be presented with a dance of stately, ritual nature, perhaps something like the rope-dance described in Livy (27. 37.12-14) as danced by young girls (cf *mollia* here, a word applied to pretty girls' arms at Ovid *AA* 1.595). *pede* here is to be understood more in terms of rhythm than physical feet (*OLD* s.v. *pes* 11b), with an obvious pun on the other sense of the word. This entails rendering *pede convenienti* as 'in a suitable rhythm' – more difficult, perhaps, than 'with the feet in harmony' but lending more point to the sarcastic description of images as 'well-trained'. *oculis* is still a problem; it is obviously theoretically inconsistent, (in that dream images do not enter by the eyes,) but may simply stand for the 'mind's eye', underlining yet again the common origins of both waking sight and sleeping dreams. Creech's *ollis* is unbearably dull!

792 **must be..:** *scilicet* introduces heavy sarcasm, as L presents a fantastic account of the images 'putting on a show' in the dark; the sense of 'illusion' comes out in the phrase *ludos facere* (which often means 'to fool or shame somebody' *OLD* s.v. *ludus* 4ab) and perhaps also in the word *madent*, which often connotes intoxication (cf. 3. 479).

138

794-6 one moment: each moment of perception can be subdivided into 'atomic' moments of imperceptibly short duration; this is the idea which underpins many of Zeno's famous paradoxes (cf Barnes ch.13), although it is not susceptible of empirical verification, being merely a mental construct. (cf Furley (1967) I ch.8).

804-5 prepares itself: the mental activity is automatic, as suggested by the repetition of *se ipse paravit/ipse parat sese*, but the control is not complete – especially in dreams (cf 818-22) – which is why it is a matter of 'hope'. The instantaneous image sent up on the mental screen is well brought out by the snappy *fit ergo*.

807-15 From the fact that concentrating on one thing often means ignoring other possible objects for our attention, L extrapolates the theory that mental images are similarly a selection from alternative images.

807-9 prepare..fine-textured: L loads the argument by using words in describing the process of vision which we have grown to associate with mental activity.

816-7 massive...minuscule: *maxima parvis* juxtaposed brings out the fallibility of our senses in a manner explained at 379-468: this follows on logically from what has gone before in that if we focus all our attention on one tiny set of images we will lose all wider perspective and thus misjudge the situation. *adopinamur* is L's word for Epicurus' *to prosdoxazomenon*, *signis* suggests *semeia* or indirect evidence used inferentially to produce conclusions about matters (e.g. astronomy) not susceptible of direct verification. (For the wider aspects of the theory of *semeia* and inference cf Sedley (1982). Used here *signis* thus suggests indirect evidence as by definition more fallible than straight perception.

818-22 To round off this section L produces a memorable passage descriptive of the incoherent nonsense which we see in dreams, to demonstrate the essential function of the memory and intellectual faculties in sorting out the images in waking life.

819-20 in our hands: unless *in manibus* is a metaphor from the plastic arts (we remould the figure of a woman into that of a man) it must refer to part of the dream itself, since the hands themselves play no part in the perception of dreams; L may have in mind an erotic dream in which the woman being embraced (*in manibus*) suddenly turns into a man.

L digresses here to argue against the common 'theological' view which saw the world as created by the gods for a purpose, a view which of course militates against his own mechanistic view of causality and chance. At 5.110–234 he argues against the divine creation of the world, at 6.379–422 he argues against the myth that thunderbolts are fired by the gods; here, as is fitting in this book about sense-perception and illusion, he rebuts the illusion that our sense-organs were created in order to perceive. There is no good evidence that L has the Stoics particularly in mind here – the views he refutes are much older than the Stoics, appearing in (e.g.) Xenophon *Memorabilia* 1.4 and Aristotle (see Furley (1966) 27).

823 we..desire: MSS *inesse* is clearly corrupt. Munro's *avessis* is palaeographically nice but philologically unlikely (*OLD* quotes no instance of this form). Most probable is Bernays' *avemus* (cf 2.216, 3.1083, 4.778)

824 you to escape: the second person pronoun is needed here (Bailey's *te fugere* for MSS *effugere*) – L has none of the preacher's mock-humility about his own salvation, as *he* knows the answer already.

827–31 The language here is scathingly ironic, terms such as 'based' (*fundata*), 'flexible', 'fastened' and 'supplied' being used with withering sarcasm to debunk the teleological view – as if those who held that view believed that men were constructed piece by piece, a set of interlocking parts screwed together like a robot. Refutation by ridicule – again.
For a similar account of creation cf Plato *Protagoras* 320d–321c.

832 Notice the violent tmesis of *inter quaecumque pretantur* indicative of the disorder of such views.

833 back to front: because such views put the cart before the horse, turning effects into causes and vice versa, as explained at 834–5.

837 language: cf 5.1028–90 on the origins of language, with Schrijvers *Mnemosyne* 27.4 (1974) 337–64.

843–54 L now contrasts man himself as a teleological animal who does invent things for a purpose (beds, drinking cups, etc.) with nature, which is not. The false notion of divine teleology arose, he seems to imply, because man applied his own characteristics to the world as a whole.

Later on (5.1350ff) L turns his anti-teleological stance into a moral stance, arguing that simple implements are just as effective as sophisticated tools, acorns are as nutritious as fine food (cf 4.630-2), and that 'progress' in living standards only makes it harder for men to be content.

845   gleaming: alludes to the development of metallurgy (cf 5.1241-80).

846   nature forced: L implies that human instincts are constant, and that only the means of fulfilling them are variable; furthermore, sophistication will only turn to frustration (5.1412-35).

847   supplied the barrier: the epic-sounding periphrasis and archaic *parmai* may be designed to evoke the long-dead warriors of very early times.

854   idea: a favourite argument with L – we cannot invent something unless we already have the concept (*notitia*); cf 476, 479; 2.745; 5.124,182,1047.

858 – 76 HUNGER

L is concerned in this section of the poem to explain the physical, mechanical cause of appetitive behaviour. So we have learnt about mental visualisation (779-817); now we are told the origins of Hunger, movement and sex. The case of hunger is straightforward – it is merely the growing of a void inside us caused by the loss of atoms (2.1118ff), whereas thirst is caused when the internal parts of the body are over-heated and need cooling. (See Introduction, pp 5-6).

858-9   nature of...body: cf 846n on instincts.

860-1   particles flow...: internal motion (*palsis*) causes the atoms on the outside surface to be thrown off.

861-2   motion: this increases the friction and collisions incurred by the body and hence increases the loss of surface atoms.

863-4   exhaled...pant: notice the heavy, tired spondees of *os exhalantur* and the panting anaphora and elision of *languida anhelant.*

866-76   A double metaphor of a collapsing building and a fire in the stomach. *subruitur* (undermined) leads to pain (*dolor*) expressed in jerky, halting rhythm (*rem* as the last syllable); at once we take corrective measures – food 'shores up' (*suffulciat*) the limbs and strengthens the

141

cracks (*interdatus*) and plugs the holes (*patentem obturet*). The metaphor is well sustained by the constant alternation of building and body (*suffulciat artus... vires interdatus... amorem obturet edendi*) (cf West (1969) 65-6).

870   all those parts: the tmesis of *quae loca cumque* suggests the scattering of the parts all over the body.

873-4   extinguishing...: note the assonance of *-stinguit ut ignem* and *amplius aridus artus*, the latter suggesting perhaps the dry scorching heat, producing the gasping sounds of thirst (*anhela sitis* 875).

875   panting: *anhela* picks up *anhelant* from 864 and sets up a nice cycle of: activity – panting – loss of atoms/concentration of heat atoms – panting – thirst.

877 - 906 MOTION AND WILL

L has explained the appetitive force of hunger and thirst in purely mechanistic terms; now he will outline the mechanics of apparently free motion, maintaining the freedom of action – if there were no free will there would be no point in preaching – while also tying the facility of movement closely with the facility of visualisation, without which 'nobody ever begins to do anything'. We are in the same predicament as at 779ff – the mind has the power to choose which images to focus upon, and so in this case can reject the image of legs walking which prompts the action, although the essence of this 'desire' is never explored or explained. (See Rist 90-99, Bailey 432-7 Furley (1967) 210-26).

880   got..into the habit: Aristotle stresses (*Nicomachean Ethics* B 3,1104b3-13) the importance of 'right training' in conditioning our responses from an early age to see that we feel pleasure when doing good (even if the 'good' is standing fast in the face of danger) and pain when doing evil; L assumes here similarly that our 'freedom' is limited by the Pavlovian conditioning which early life may have imposed upon us, and that what applies to the mere mechanics of walking might take on a moral significance if that walking was desertion of the battlefield or burglary of someone's house. See Furley (1967) 222-5, and the implications of 1280-87 below.

881-91 The sequence of events is: images of walking present themselves to the mind (*animus*)- if it wishes the body to move it sends the message to the spirit (*anima*) spread, like the nervous system, throughout the body – the *anima* then instructs the limbs to move.

886   mind stirs itself: unashamedly active verb expressing free volition.

887-8   spirit: L has no problem of mind/body dualism such as has plagued many philosophers, because he admits of no distinction in material substance between the two. The spirit is a two-way transmitter: it feels e.g. a spider crawling on the hand, and it then tells the hand to squash it.

889   close connection: cf 3.136.

891   mass is slowly...: a slow spondaic line expressive of the laborious effort; cf 902.

892-906   L now produces one of his more extravagant theories. He has already argued (865) that movement causes animals to lose atoms and thus 'rarefy'; he now asserts that the widened pores consequent on this rarefaction would act like sails on a ship, be filled with air and thus aid the body in its movement. cf 6.1031-3.

896   two things: that is, the limbs and the air (corresponding to the ship and the sails).

899   such minute..so large: notice the effective juxtaposition and chiasmus of *tantula..tantum corpus corpuscula*; cf 902 *magnam magno*.

902-3   massive...one single..: after the heavy m alliteration and spondaic rhythm of 902, 903 is lively and swift, pointing the contrast between the heavy ship and the agile hand.

906   gentle push: the principle of the lever, well shown in the contrast between the heavy machinery of 905 and the effortless verbs of 906.

907 – 61 SLEEP

If sensation is produced by contact with the *anima* or spirit, then this spirit must be disconnected in sleep; the spirit atoms cannot, however, be totally disturbed, or we would never wake up again (cf 3.607-14 on slow death). As the *anima* atoms are located both on the surface of the body (where they pick up contact with other bodies and images) and also inside the body – where they act as a link with the mind – the disconnection must occur in both places. The common factor in both is air – breathed into the inside of the body, encountered also against the surface skin. The constant battering of the air causes the spirit atoms to lose their coherence. Bailey well points out that L sees the essential feature of sleep as being anaesthesia; the mind is still awake in dreams, the bodily organs are still functioning involuntarily – it is only the awareness of sensation which is dormant. cf. Schrijvers (1976).

909–11 verses...: cf 180–2n.
914 you go away...: notice the word-order – *vera'* *repulsanti[2] discedas[3] pectore[2] dicta'*.
914–5 you..are to blame: cf 5.1425. Notice also how it is a matter of 'discerning the truth', continuing L's constant motif that the senses are reliable if only we look properly.
919 lose their tension...: this reverses the order of 908, where the flowing comes before the relaxation.
920 consciousness..spirit: already demonstrated at 3.238–51, 269–72. The argument is:
     spirit produces sensation.
     no sensation entails no spirit.
but no spirit = death. ∴ partial loss of spirit.
924 soaked in the eternal...: this epic-sounding line well conveys the immutable finality of death with its sonorous ring, after the staccato phrases of 923. It also sets up the theme of life = fire, death = cold which L takes up 926–8.
926–8 fire: a convincing analogy to the theory of the spirit. Some of the fire leaves as smoke and heat and flames, some of it dies down into smouldering embers; just as the spirit is partly emitted, partly condensed down deep into the body. (see West (1969) 87–9).
931 winds: cf Otto s.v. *ventus* 2.
934 thumped...beaten: L loads the case with violent verbs to evoke the heavy collision of the body with the air; cf also 938.
935–6 for this reason: these lines seem at first sight inconsistent with L's anti-teleological stance (823–57); but in fact L does not assert a *purpose* behind the hides, merely the brute fact that things without such protection do not survive, as at 5.855–77.
937–8 flogs in respiration: this suggests that L is thinking of sleep following hard exercise which has already (862–6) been described as 'rarifying' the body.

939 thrashed: *vapulet* is a comic word (Plautus *As*.404, *Aul*.457, *Rud*.1401, Seneca *Apoc*.15.2) creating the picture of a hapless slave flogged whichever way he turns.

940 blows pierce: the marked p alliteration evokes the sensation of the blows slapping against the body.

942 gradual demolition: sleep is regarded as a gradual process, whereas waking up is sudden (927). The imagery here is that of a house being demolished (cf 950ff), just as hunger was similarly described; it is ironic that the demolition of hunger is repaired by food, but eating is a prime cause of *this* demolition of sleep (866ff: 954-61)

944-9 L does not explain how we ever manage to wake up. In particular, the spirit atoms which are expelled from the body would be hard to recall; nor does L explain what process re-connects the disconnected *anima* inside the body. Boyancé's theory that the atoms expelled are recalled into the body in breathing is clearly wrong, since breathing is one of the means of destroying the coherence of the *anima* which brings on sleep in the first place. (Boyancé 205; cf. Schrijvers (1976) 247).

948 barricades: the tmesis of *inter enim saepit* is a verbal recreation of the physical dismemberment.

950 prop up: the spirit is often seen as something like a skeleton which holds up the body erect, such that sleep and death leave it 'poured out' (3.112) on the ground. L describes the sleeper in terms reminiscent of puppets when the strings have been cut.

954 air: any invasion of the inside of the body, whether it is air in breathing or food in eating, causes a displacement of the *anima* atoms, which explains why sleep follows work or food, since work induces panting (864-5) which both disturbs the *anima* itself and also induces eating which disturbs the *anima* further – which finally induces sleep.

959 partial: adverbial *parte* (OQ) is less well-attested than Lachmann's *partim*.

959-60 thrusting down..expulsion: note the chiastic antithesis of *coniectus altior..foras eiectus*.

L has already discussed dreams as a form of mental illusion (453-61) and in particular he has singled out dreams of the dead several times, to counter the superstitious belief in ghosts and fear of death (cf 26-44n). In the present passage he is concerned to explain dreams in terms of images; dreams can thus be explained entirely in naturalistic terms, without recourse to any of the supernatural interpretations which are put upon them (cf Cicero *de div*. I.30.63). The dreams of animals are brought in for this very reason - to prove that dreams have no prophetic or magical functions, but are merely the mechanical reaction of the mind to the images presented to it. The phenomenon of 'occupational' dreams which recapitulate events of the day is so obvious as to need explaining; L thus argues that our 'enthusiasm and pleasure' (984) lead us, even in sleep, to focus on those images most familiar to us - or indeed most worrying to us, as in the cases of dreamers indicting themselves by talking in their sleep (1018-9) or dreamers terrified by imaginary wild beasts (1016-7). All of this seems to contradict L's earlier statement (765) that the memory lies dormant in sleep - if that were so, we could not relive our past lives in dreams; what L clearly means is that images from the past are still appearing to us, and our natural inclinations direct us towards some of these, although our critical faculties, born of our conscious memory of what is possible, are dormant. On this whole passage cf Schrijvers (1980).

962-3 **addicted..time:** L distinguishes two causes of recurrent dreams - obsessional interest and the length of time spent over a given activity.

966 **matching law...:** *componere leges* may also mean to 'collate' laws. The 'etymological' repetition of *causidici causas* is in 'the rhetorical style of the lawyer's courtroom' (Snyder 79).

968 **waging a war:** *vellum* (O) and *velum* (Q) are clearly wrong, and the obvious correction is that of P, *bellum* (cf 5.1289). *duellum* is read by Bailey, although the synizesis ought to cause comment. The archaism of *induperatores* is Ennian, as is *duellum* (cf Ennius frag. 559 and 565, where both *duellis* and *induperator* occur). This makes the archaism *duellum* look more certain, suggesting that the whole line is a parody of earlier epic.

contractum may carry the undertone (*OLD* s.v. *contraho* 6b) of commercial dealings, appropriate to sailors engaged in trade.

969–70 **I dream:** after three end-stopped lines, L expands into a couplet. His 'poet's dream' is quite unlike the apparitions enjoyed by Ennius, Propertius, Callimachus and others; in contrast to their supernatural fantasies, L's dream is naturalistic and real (cf Schrijvers (1980) 141).

973–83 This is the fourth passage in this book to treat of the theatre (cf 74–83, 768–772, 788–93), and theatrical metaphors are yet to come (cf e.g. 1186). As Schrijvers hints (1980) 142, the theatre forms 'a small but fitting *Leitmotiv* in the book concerned with sense-perception'. The theatre is both analogical to our perception of the world in general (we only see the surface facade, etc.) and also exemplifies features of our perception (e.g. colour (74–83)) which the poet wishes to explain.
Roman Games tended to last at least a week (*ludi Cereales*) if not a fortnight (*ludi Romani*); cf Carcopino 224–5.

976 **channels:** L attempts to explain the mechanics of short-term habit or memory in terms of specific channels opened up which fit the specific images of the theatre perfectly. cf Diogenes of Oenoanda NF 5.III. 6–14, quoted by Smith (Loeb edition p. 353).

979 **even...awake:** L's description (980–3) of movement, music, bright light (*splendere*) and colour (*varios*) is compared by Schrijvers ((1980) 142–3) to Aristotle *De insomniis* 459b12ff.

980 **dancers:** cf 788–91n.

981 **fluent song:** this is a highly musical line – appropriately – with chiastic sound pattern of *liquidum carmen chordasque loquentis,* the c alliteration suggesting the sound of the 'speaking strings' being plucked, and the interchange of epithets in *liquidum* (more appropriate to sound than words) and *loquentis* (more appropriate to song than strings).

984 **pleasure:** *voluptas* (Lachmann) is almost certainly right for MSS *voluntas*. Most of us find it impossible to direct our dreaming as we want – cf L's examples of morbid dreaming at 1013–23 – and yet there *is* considerable importance in pleasure as a motive force for dreams of particular kinds (cf 1030–6 for an obvious example).

986   **not only humans**: picks up *hominum* 972, to correct it.

987-1010   L examines animal behaviour at length to prove that if animals experience the same dreams as men - granted that other people's dreams cannot be conclusively verified but only inferred from 'signs' (cf 816-7n) - then dreams are no more supernatural or strange than anything else. Epicurean theory saw animals as the 'mirrors of nature', which allow us to identify the common instincts and characteristics which unite us with other living things.

988   **sweating..panting**: the s alliteration suggests the panting of the horse.

990   **racing off**: *saepe quiete* (OQ) is obviously taken from 991, leaving us no palaeographical data to work from in emending it. Suggestions have accordingly been many. What L is hinting at presumably is the sudden jerk of a sleeping racehorse as if it were suddenly released from the stall at the start of the race. Pricking up ears, moving limbs, stretching legs, wanting to fly, are all senseless conjectures - for what distinguishes a limb-movement or an ear-prick in the starting-stall from the same movement somewhere else? We only *see* the sleeping horse, we cannot read its mind, so whatever L wrote must have indicated movement which looked like the start of the race. (Martin's *edere voces* is embarrassingly silly - horses do not shout when starting a race, or at least I know of no distinctive race-starting neigh recognisable by connoisseurs). The only conjectures which fit are: *membra movere* (Bouterwerk), *rumpere sese* (M.F. Smith) and *fundere sese* (Richter). The latter two are preferable on grounds of vividness; and *fundere* seems to have been the *mot juste* for precisely this situation, from parallels e.g. Ennius *Ann*.484, V.*Geor*. 1.512; 3.104.

991   **dogs**: cf 5.1063-72 for L's observation of hunting dogs. L enlivens his account here by the emphasis given to *iactant* and *mittunt* at the beginning of their respective lines, suggesting the sudden jerk and the sudden bark.

995   **awoken**: the dream remains even after the dogs have woken up. This is put in to emphasise again the common nature of waking experience and dreams, without implausible accounts of *ourselves* chasing phantoms.

997   **illusions**: *erroribus* refers literally to the dogs' futile wandering off after a non-existent stag. The metaphor of 'shaking off wanderings' is bold.

999 rush: *instant* has the senses of: to take a stand against (*OLD* s.v. *insto* 4), to threaten (cf 1.65), and to apply oneself urgently to something. All three senses are vivid in the Latin.

1000–1003 = 992–5 and must be excluded.

1004 faces and forms: *facies atque ora* is vivid, not tautological; the dog first sees the general appearance (*facies*), then the actual face (*ora*) of the stranger.

1005–6 the rougher: the ferocity of dreams is proportional to the ferocity of species – which in turn is dependent on the proportions of the wind, heat and air in their spirits (3.288–306) – as is also the case with man (3.307–22).

1008–10 groves of the gods: L sets up a strong contrast between the birds' *real* situation – the proverbially peaceful groves of the gods (cf 3.18–22 for the tranquillity of the abodes of the gods) – and their *imaginary* perilous predicament (well evoked by the confused phrasing of 1010, the asyndeton *proelia pugnas*, the alliteration of p and v). There may also be a slight jest at the expense of any 'sanctuary' the birds expected to find in divine groves: Epicurus' gods do not concern themselves about men, still less birds.

1011–23 L returns to human dreams, quickly moving into a brief description of anxiety-dreams, a form of experience known to Homer (cf Dodds 106) and lending support to the 'psychopathological' significance of dreams (Schrijvers (1980) 139–40). Many of the 'literary' dreams well-known to L's readers take this morbid and/or revelatory form (e.g. Clytemnestra's dream (Aeschylus *Choephoroi* 32–41, Sophocles *Electra* 417–23) Astyages' dream about Mandane (Herodotus 1.108)) and thus L's treatment of the phenomenon is no evidence of psychological derangement on the part of the poet, as suggested by Perelli 265–6.

1011–2 great deeds: these lines are grandiose (notice the enjambment emphasising *magna*, the prolix tautology *faciuntque geruntque*), leading to the rapid sequence of vivid verbs in 1013ff, suggestive of the suddenness and violence of the dream-images.

1013 kings: *reges* could be nominative or accusative – but the 'royal dream' is so common in literature (see Schrijvers (1980) 146, Dodds 109) and the dream-like suddenness of the reversal from storming a city to being captured themselves is so effective, that it is most probably nominative.

1014   then and there: *ibidem* is ironic - all these gruesome events happen while they lie quite still.

1015-20   many: the fourfold repetition of *multi* serves to convince the reader that such 'psychopathological' dreams are really very common.

1016   panther: a staple feature of gladiatorial shows was the *venatio* (hunt) in which men would fight against bulls, panthers, lions, leopards and tigers. (cf Carcopino 260-1) L does not necessarily confine these dreams to the gladiators themselves - if the audience found it hard to dispel the innocuous sights described at 980-3, then *a fortiori* wild-beast hunts must have left an impression.

1017   screams: notice the howling assonance of *mandantur magnis...- oribus omnia complent.*

1018-9   talk..in sleep: cf 5.1158-60. As examples of such 'conscience-dreams' Schrijvers quotes Sallust's Catiline 'unable to rest either awake or asleep' (Sall. *Cat.* 15.4) and King Philip's nightmare at Polybius 18.15 and 23.10.

1022-3   terrified: L may be thinking of the common experience in which the dreamer imagines he is falling and wakes up with a start *before* he 'dies'; he is in any case not counting these dreamers among those who *mortem obeunt*, and the long descriptive phrase *de montibus...toto* is abruptly ended with the sharp *exterruntur. mentibu' capti* is legalese for 'insane' - cf Cicero *de Officiis* 27.94.

1023   return to their senses: *ad se redire* was recently (997) used of dogs.

1024-36   L now passes from psychological to physical explanations of dreams, such that physical stimuli produce appropriate dreams (cf Aristotle *Div.somn* 463a 10ff). L's sequence of thirst - bedwetting - nocturnal ejaculation is mentally, if not biologically, coherent.

1024-5   thirsty: the thirsty man (*sitiens*) is verbally surrounded by the water he dreams of; the extravagance of 'virtually the whole stream' is suitably dream-like and enhanced by the gaping vowel of *faucibus*.

1026   children: why 'clean' persons should be inclined to wet the bed is a mystery, but the MSS *puri* has been retained by a surprising number of editors. It is obvious from *tum quibus* (1030) that L sees bed-wetting as a feature of childhood developing into the superficially similar phenomenon of nocturnal ejaculation, but *puri* is unattested in the sense of 'innocents, i.e. children'. L's phrasing in these lines corroborates the sense of 'children'; *dolia* are large storage-vessels used to contain liquids or grain, but nowhere else used of chamber-pots, and *curta* (short, low) suggests that the persons urinating are too short themselves to use the full-size model – the childish prank of urinating in a wine-jar is thus cleverly turned against the children themselves as they soak their bedclothes. Clarke suggests *parvi*, which is admirable for all the considerations outlined above.

028   filtered: a *saccus* was a filter used to strain wine and other things – there is thus a nice irony about the 'filtered' liquid flowing into the wine-jar.

029   Babylonian: brilliantly coloured, expensive cloth. The proverbial inability of children to show respect for the expensive is brought out by the bathos of the sonorous *Babylonica magnifico splendore* being soaked.

030   rough seas: an excellent metaphor for adolescence.

031   time: *dies* is also effective in suggesting that the seed is built up in the day to be released at night.

032   any and every body: in contrast to the besotted lover, the adolescent is indiscriminate in his desire. .

033   heralding: the images are 'messengers' of the desired body; later on (1095) L stresses the futility of love in that we *only* have images to enjoy.
complexion: the favoured complexion was evidently fair-skinned; cf *OLD* s.v. *candidus* 5a.

034   parts: *loca* here must mean 'penis', which is both linguistically (cf Adams 95) unusual and biologically strange – did L believe that the penis is swollen with sperm?

035   the whole job: *rebus* here standing for *rebus veneriis*, a euphemism for sexual intercourse; it may also suggest 'a happy holiday from the "business" concerns cited at the beginning of the paragraph (966–70)' (Fitzgerald, 75).

036   flood of a massive river: 'an ejaculation of almost cosmically generous proportions' (Fitzgerald *ibid*). It is clear from the exaggeration that L is speaking from the dreamer's fantastic viewpoint; Horace's emission (*Sat.* 1.5.84–5) is far more mundane.

151

The coherence of this whole final section is unwelcome to those critics who see L as a deranged misogynist or a sadistic pervert, ignoring the fact that the last 78 lines of the book are positive instruction conducive to sexual happiness and fertility; and those critics who actually read these final lines often assert that in them L is untrue to Epicurus' teaching on marriage. Both points merit consideration.

Epicurus' attitude to sex was ambivalent. In one place (D.L.10.118) he says that 'sexual intercourse has never done a man good, and he is lucky if it hasn't done him harm', in another he counts sexual pleasure among the good things of life (D.L.10.6). To understand the sense behind the apparent contradiction one has to remember that the highest good for Epicurus was *ataraxia*, serenity and freedom from all disturbance; if the calculus of good is the amount of disturbance avoided, then sexual indulgence will be good insofar as it releases the disturbance of frustration, bad if it encroaches on overall serenity of disposition. This distinction is brought out in L's dichotomy of the *sani* and the *miseri*, the healthy and the wretched. The pathetic delusions of the infatuated lover are stigmatised as 'sick' and 'mad' (1068–9nn), whereas the quieter charms of the 'homely little woman' are enunciated with approval and the 'habit of love' sounds very much like Epicurean friendship (1278–87; cf Cicero *Fin*.1.21.69). Sexual pleasure itself seems to have fallen into the second class of pleasures categorised by Epicurus, viz those which are natural but not necessary, and hence are to be satisfied only in moderation (unlike necessary pleasures such as eating, and unnatural, unnecessary pleasures such as luxury; cf Epicurus *Men*.127, *K.D*.29, Cic. *Fin*.1.45). If one remembers also that in Epicurean doctrine pleasure cannot be increased once natural desires are satisfied, but only varied (see *Men*.130–1, *K.D*.3,18, Cic.*Fin*.1.38), then L's attitude to sex becomes clearly descriptive rather than prescriptive: we do not *in fact* enjoy the 'life of love' of the romantic, our sexual needs can be satisfied just as well (if not better – cf 1073–6) in promiscuous encounters as they can in the obsessive attachment to one girl – a nice example of the *parvum quod satis est* argument (enough is as good as a feast) found at e.g. 2.20–36, 5.1412–35. The moderate indulgence of sexual pleasure demanded by our bodies can be gratified and enjoyed without the pain of romantic infatuation.

For L makes it abundantly clear that the sexual urge is natural; we have seen that perception is the result of effluences beyond our control, and we have seen the non-voluntary phenomena of hunger, sleep and dreams explained in strictly atomic terms. When sex is introduced, therefore, it is already in a context of mechanical atomic reactions over which we have little control and with which we have to come to terms. (Aristotle also (*de motu animalium* 703b 5ff) discusses the movement of the penis along with sleeping and waking and breathing as movements over which we have no control; cf Furley (1967) 221-2). The emission of sperm is thus necessary and natural; what is unnecessary and unnatural is the *retention* of sperm as practised by the obsessed lover (1065-7n). Marriage is assumed (*nostris* 1277), and assumed to be designed for procreation (1264-8) with a wife who is of 'compliant ways' (1281) – all of which is easy enough to obtain. The romantic lover is doomed to inevitable frustration because his illusions and expectations do not allow him to see the truth and realise 'what is the limit of possession, to what extent real pleasure can grow' (5.1432-3). His love-making is therefore greedy, blind and unsatisfied – as un-Epicurean as can be imagined. It is these unhealthy aspects of sex which Epicurus and L condemn. (On this passage see Betensky, Goar, Kleve, Taladoire, Fitzgerald etc.)

1037-57 The secretion and ejaculation of sperm. Notice that L only explores male sexuality here – but 1211ff makes it clear that he believed that women also emit seed. In this passage L treats sexual desire as the mechanical response of the body to the outside stimulus of a beautiful body and the internal stimulus of the build-up of sperm; the 'urge' (*voluntas*) is an atomic reaction no less than hunger (858-76), which makes the mythological 'blows of Venus' (1052) sarcastic in intention.

1038 <u>stiffens</u>: *roborat* has the primary sense here of 'strengthen': as the sperm is taken from all over the body (*corpore toto* 1042) it is only when the whole body is strong that it can be spared; there may also be a *double entendre* intended.

1040 <u>human</u>: note the threefold repetition of *homine humanum hominis*, and observe that the fair sex may be male or female (cf 1053n).

1041 <u>abodes</u>: Democritus and Epicurus held that sperm is drawn from the whole body, as also did Hippocrates (*De* gen. 8); Plato (*Timaeus* 91 ab) however believed that sperm is the 'marrow which comes from the head along the spine'. *eiectum..exit* is picked up by *eicere* at 1046; the sexual process is a series of ejections – first of the 'seeds' from their 'abodes', then of the 'collected liquid' (1065) out of the body.

1043 groin: for the uses of *nervus* (literally 'sinew, tendon') meaning 'penis' see Adams 38.
specific: *certa* again (cf 87n, 1225) indicates the mechanical, automatic sequence.

1046-57 L describes sex in the language of the battlefield: *contendit... petit.. saucia... cadunt in vulnus*, and especially 1050-1, where the parallel is made explicit. The theme of the warfare of love has already been adumbrated at 1.34, where Mars (god of war) lies 'conquered by the eternal wound of love', and was a favourite of the Greek erotic poets (see Kenney (1970) 380-5). L thus appears to be using the language of romantic love against itself – a device he will use constantly from here to 1191. L's attack in this passage takes the form of spelling out in real, not to say crude, terms, just what the 'romantics' are talking about when they use metaphors.

1046 awful: on the use of *dira* cf A. Traina 260-66.

1049-51 The soldier falls towards the source of the wound and 'ejaculates' blood; the lover does the same and ejaculates semen. L 'deromanticises' sex with the vivid physical detail of 'red fluid soaks our enemy', at the same time pointing to the irony that we 'love' that which is our enemy.

1052 blows of Venus: the cliché deserves to be put in inverted commas – and serves to underline the parallel with warfare again.

1053 boy with womanish limbs: intense romantic love between males (such as we find in e.g. Plato's *Symposium* 183a) was comparatively rare in Rome, but casual pederasty was quite acceptable and by no means the same thing as effeminacy (cf J. Griffin (1976) 100-2). Love of boys is recommended by Propertius (2.4.17-22) for its lack of emotional complication, although the connoisseur Ovid (*Ars am.* 2.683-4) thinks it inferior to love of women in terms of pleasure; and the figure of the *puer delicatus* (fancy boy) is common in Roman social life – cf Trimalchio's grotesque catamite at Petronius *Sat.* 64.5-6 – without ever impugning the virility of the master. This only applied to the pursuit of boys (and 'womanish' suggests pre-pubertal at that) and not men – cf Ovid's stinging remark at *Ars Am.* 1.524 about 'fake men who try to attract men'. L does not expand on the theme of romantic love between man and boy, presumably because such love was rare (though cf Tibullus 1.9, with Lyne 173-4); this boy is clearly only seen as a surrogate woman (*muliebribus...mulier*).

1054 whole body: cf 1172. Notice also the word-play whereby *iactans amorem* (sending out love) leads inexorably to *iacere umorem* (ejaculating fluid).

1056 body..body: the juxtaposition of *corpus de corpore* verbalises the intimate proximity of the bodies.

1057 dumb...pleasure: lust is seen as purely a physical urge, the mind playing no part in it, the sole instinct being the pull of pleasure. (cf Euripides *Troades* 990, where Aphrodite (goddess of love) is punned with *aphrosyne* (thoughtlessness)).

1058-60 Venus...name: *cupido* (1057) means 'desire', and is also the name of Venus' winged son Cupid who injects desire with his arrows. Notice the tricolon crescendo of *haec... hinc... hinc,* and the slightly pejorative tone of *illaec* ('that old cliché of...') introducing the tired idea of love dripping into the heart, only to freeze. Editors quote Eur. *Hipp.* 525-6, rightly; but Fitzgerald (76 n.12) plausibly suggests that L is thinking of a stalagmite growing upwards (*successit*) from underneath dripping water; 'it would be characteristic of L's satirical style if he were visualising in this concrete fashion Euripides' image...' – and notice the ambiguous sense of *cura*, a word used often in love poetry of the beloved herself – who will hardly be flattered by the description *frigida.* (Kleve 378, compares Philodemus *Epig.* VIII.4 (*AP* 10.21)).

1061 images: the Epicurean theory of perception, expounded in this book, dooms the lover to perpetual teasing from the beloved; nor are these the interchangeable images of 'any and every body' (1032) – *illius* lingers on in wistful enjambment, and her name is singular and 'sweet' (cf Prop.1.12.6).

1063 feed: the metaphor of *pabula* (fodder) is picked up at 1068 (*alendo* – 'if it is nourished'). Again L translates the poetic *amoris* into the blunt *umorem* (1065); we should flee from love (*amorem*) by expelling fluid (*umorem*).

1065-7   L sees romantic love as bred of sexual frustration: the lover's physical desire is sublimated into an idealisation of the beloved, such as scholars have found in Medieval literature (cf Sarsby 21-2). This is corroborated later on (1177-84) by the figure of the 'locked-out lover' who would flee if he were admitted, as his idealised portrait, bred of physical distance, would be crudely disillusioned.

1065   indiscriminately: cf 1071. This was also the advice of the elder Cato, according to Porphyry on Horace *Sat.* 1.2 and seems well in accord with traditional Roman attitudes to (male) sexuality - see Lyne 1-4.

1067   inevitable pain: good Epicurean considerations - pain is to be avoided *per se*, and like all else it is an inexorable part of the mechanical process described. Note that the theme of pain is developed later (1080-2) in the act of love itself, the pain of sickness (love) leading to the infliction of pain on the beloved.

1068   sore: the notion of love as a disease is also found at Catullus 76.20; both poets were drawing on a theme from Greek literature - cf Sophocles *Trach.* 445, Euripides *Hipp* 477 (with Barrett *ad loc*). Only L extends the theme into an ethical consideration and a serious piece of practical advice to the reader.

1069   madness: again, this is paralleled in Greek literature (see esp. Plato *Timaeus* 91b7 *oistrodeis*), but is turned by L into a rich source of philosophical coherence, in that the essence of madness to the ancients was hallucination (cf Sophocles *Ajax*, Euripides *Heracles*, in both of which the madness is *not* the violence but the mistaking of innocent victims for the real enemies); thus at the close of this book which has concerned itself above all with perception and scepticism it is supremely relevant to see illusion to the point of madness and its disastrous results (1121ff).

1070   confound..wounds: there may be an allusion in *conturbes* to Catullus 5.11 - see Betensky 296 n.22. The paradox of fighting old wounds with new blows is striking and effective.

1071   sexual promiscuity: *vulgivaga Venus* is probably taken from Callimachus' word *periphoitos* used 'in rejection of the promiscuous beloved' (*Ep.* 28.3; Brown (1982) 89).

1072   in another direction: in accordance with Epicurus' sanguine advice: 'remove sight and...contact and the passion of love is ended' (*Sent.Vat.* 18).

1073-4 enjoyment of sex: casual sex has no penalties attached
to it (such as L outlines at 1121-40) and is also more
conducive to pleasure than romantic attachment, as the
pleasure is *pura* (uncontaminated by illusions and futile
expectations). L contrasts here the healthy (*sanis*) with
the sick (*miseris*), continuing the ideas of *ulcus* (1068),
dolorem (1067) and *vulnera* (1070); Kleve (379-80)
stresses that this idea reconciles the apparently
conflicting Epicurean ideas of love; on the true canon of
pleasure vs pain, love may be a source of pleasure (to
the healthy) or pain (to the sick, i.e. infatuated). It is
only unhealthy, morbid attachments which Epicurus
renounced.
1076-8 even in..possession: L creates a picture of sex in
which the lover is so frenzied that he cannot make up his
mind what to enjoy first – like a child spoilt for choice –
to suggest that they do not really enjoy anything
properly.
1077 burning passion: a metaphor extended at 1086-7. Cf also
1.473-7, where the 'fire' of Paris' love led to the real fire
of Troy.
1079-81 pain: cf 1067n. L's language here is deliberately
provocative, interweaving the affectionate words of love
(the diminutive *labellis; oscula*) with verbs of violence –
illidere dentem occurs at Hor.*Sat.* 2.1.77 (used there of
envy), *illisit* is more at home in the boxing match of
V.*Aen.* 5.480. The romantic conceit of the love-bite (cf
Cat.8.18) is transformed into a morbid psychosis. (Cf
Traina 267-8; N-H ad H.*Od.* 1.13.11.).
1080 bite: notice the hard sound of *dentes inlidunt*.
1081 mouths: *osculum* in love poetry usually means 'kiss'; it is
only with the crash of *adfligunt* (more appropriate to a
head-butt) that the sense of 'mouths' becomes clear.
1082 goad: a brilliant touch. The lover is 'hurt' into
love-making in which he hurts his beloved, a vicious
circle of pain; the phrase also suggests the slavery of
love, the 'mistress' (literally) torturing him like an
animal. Notice also the impersonal *id* – the lover is blind
in his helpless addiction to his love.
1083 madness: cf 1069n.
1085 reins in the bites: the lover is like a horse – the reins
slacken, so he loosens his bite on the bit in his mouth.
1086-7 flame: cf 1077n.

1089-90 however much we have: the comparable desire for food and drink – suggested perhaps by the reminiscence of 871-3 in 1086-7 – is caused by a physical need which can be satisfied. The mere build-up of sperm can also easily be relieved (1030-6); what cannot be satisfied is the extravagant hope of the infatuated lover caricatured at 1110-12.

1093 desire for water and bread..easily: the quasi-Homeric phrase *laticum frugumque cupido* (cf e.g. Homer *Iliad* 1.469) combines with *facile* (easily) to suggest the age-old ease of satisfying hunger and thirst.

1094 looks...complexion: images only communicate shape and colour (cf e.g. 243).

1096 insubstantial: *tenvia* is stressed by the enjambment and the following pause. The MSS *raptat* is surely a correction of *raptast* by a scribe who took *quae* to be neuter plural with *simulacra*. *spes* picks up the general sense of *fruendum* and also the ominous *tenvia, spes misella* well conveying the sense of 'forlorn hope'. Cf Otto s.v. *ventus*.

1097-1100 thirsty: cf 1024-5. The key-word *umor* is used again to link this with sex – the *umor* ejaculated in sex (1056) is not capable of quenching the fire of passion (1086-7) any more than the images of *umor* can quench the dreamer's thirst.

1099 in vain: *simulacra petit frustraque laborat* is a catalogue of frustration, extended by the verbal placing of the thirst (*sitit*) in the middle of the river (*medioque..torrenti*) and the paradox of *potans* poised at the end of the line – he is drinking and yet he is still thirsty.

1102-14 The lover wants not merely to enjoy, but to possess the beloved – L caricatures this with the ludicrous picture of lovers removing parts of the body, or attempting to disappear into the body, of their beloved.

1103 remove...delicate: the juxtaposition of *teneris abradere* heightens the effect.

1105-6 flower of youth: an odd euphemism; cf 1038, *OLD* s.v. *flos* 8a.

1107 sowing..female fields: cf 1272-3. The metaphor is common – see Adams 82-5.

1108-11: After the metaphors of 1105-7, L now becomes extravagantly specific; singular *corpus* may suggest the unity of the two bodies, *avide...salivas* certainly connotes the idea of eating greedily (cf 1091-1100), and the quasi-medical specificity of *iungunt salivas oris* (mingle the saliva of their mouth) lends an ironic distance to the description. 'Get right inside that body' is the language of Aristophanic excess and grotesquerie.

1115 lust: *cupido* is here metonymic for sperm; for *nervis* cf 1043n.

1118 object for their lust: *quod cupiant* (OQ) is the correct reading, taking the subjunctive as a relative final clause ('something for them to desire') in the manner of Ovid *Ars Am*.1.35 *quod amare velis reperire labora* ('affecting the dry and unemotional tone of a technical treatise' comments Hollis *ad loc*).

1119 trouble: their confusion is suggested by the tangled word-order of the line.

1120 secret sore: love as disease again (cf 1068n) and now blind (*caecus*) as well as dumb (1057) - *caecus* meaning both blind and also unseen; cf V.*Aen*.4.1-2.

1121-40 The price of love. It is obvious that L is here referring to obsessive 'romantic' love which takes over the lover's whole life, and his condemnation is couched in terms close to those of Cicero (*pro Caelio* 42) whose view of love as essentially *otium* - fine in its place but not to be allowed to interfere with *negotium* - is typically Roman.

1122 under the control: it would be tempting to read into this a reference to the elegists' stance of *servitium amoris*, the self-humiliating slavery of the lover towards his mistress (cf Lyne *CQ* 29 (1979) 117-30; Kenney (1970) 389), but, as Lyne points out (*art.cit*.121), L would have introduced the specific idea of enslavement if such an idea were current at the time - as also would Horace in *Sat*.1.2. The lover in this case is wholly obsessed with one woman, which means that her response is all he cares about - which will automatically place him under her control. L is voicing the attitude found also in e.g. Sophocles *Trach* 70-1, where, if Heracles endured slavery to the woman Omphale, he would endure anything, and Democritus (DK B 111, quoted by Bailey) 'the worst insult for a man would be to be governed by a woman'. The word *nutu* (literally 'nod') is comic exaggeration, suggestive of the all-powerful nod of Homer's Zeus (Homer *Iliad* 1.524-7), *aetas* perhaps suggests the waste of youth, squandered on one woman.

1123-40 The details of this passage are the stuff of Roman
Comedy (see Rosivach), a standard element of which is
the figure of the young man wasting his father's money
on a girl. This should not, however, lead to the
conclusion that 'L seems..to have drawn his exemplum
from literature and not from life' (Rosivach 403) merely
because the commodities are Greek - see Griffin (1976)
for the evidence that the stuff of Roman literature was
also the stuff of Roman life.

1123 Babylonian: cf 1029n.

1124 responsibilities: Cicero (de Officiis 1.2.4) declares that
'in fulfilling our officium (duty, responsibility) rests all
that is honourable, in its neglect lies all that is base'.
L's imagery here suggests that the lover allows his sense
of duty to deteriorate over a period of time.

1125 perfumes...Sikyon: editors have taken exception to
perfumes laughing on the feet, although in the context of
male humiliation rident is highly appropriate. unguenta
are at least expensive (see Richter 93 n.1) and, like
coverlets and slippers, typify the kind of extravagant
presents the lover would buy. This, and the startling
image of the perfumes and slippers joining in the mockery
of the man who bought them, are too effective to emend
away. On Sikyonian slippers see now Audrey Griffin 32
n.2; their status as luxury items is confirmed by Lucian
Dial.Mer.14.2, quoting a price of two drachmas, 'the
equivalent of two nights with a call-girl'.

1126 emeralds: cf Barone 77.

1127 sea-dyed: thalassina only occurs here, and clearly refers
to the purple dye obtained from the shellfish murex
brandaris; clothes dyed this colour were a byword for
regal opulence.

1128 drinks the sweat: after the haute couture of 1125-7 L
surprises us with the bathos of 1128 - the obsessive
(adsidue) lover soon finds his finery threadbare and
sweaty.

1129-32 Rosivach quotes many parallels of the young lover
squandering his inheritance on such things from comedy,
e.g. Terence Ad.117 Plautus Most. 295 (cf Segal 203-4).
For the currency of Greek terms in luxury dress and
coiffure see J. Griffin (1976) 92-3.

1129 hairbands, head-dresses: anadema is a very rare term,
being a transliteration from Greek, but is probably the
same as diadema, an ornamental headband decorated with

gold and jewels (Isidorus *Orig.* 19.31.1), very similar to the *mitra* (cf also Paoli 106). *Anth.Pal* 5.199 is very close in atmosphere to this passage.

1130 Malta and Cos: *atque Alidensia* (OQ) is very probably corrupt. The editors' explanation that the goods came from Alinda in Caria is unsatisfactory for two reasons: 1) Alinda would not produce an adjective *alidensus* with a short a 2) there is no evidence of textile-production in Alinda (cf most recently Louis Robert *Fouilles d'Amyzon* (1983) which makes it abundantly clear that Alinda produced olives and nothing else). Lambinus' proposal *ac Melitensia* is far more plausible – cf Varro *Men.* 433, Cic. *Verr.*2.176 ('I declare that you ... exported a great deal of Maltese cloth...') 4.103 (Verres turned Melita into a factory for the weaving of women's dresses). Maltese cloth probably had the fashionable erotic transparency of *Coae vestes* (see below) – see Cic *Verr.*5.27. *Chiaque* is likewise a mystery, but the most obvious emendation is *Coaque* (Bergk); 'the favourite stuffs of Cynthia and her sisters were... and the see-through *Coae vestes*' (J. Griffin (1976) 92 + n.1). There may be more to the significance of the transparency than has been recognised: cf Hor.*Sat.* 1.2.101-2, where the advantage of Coan silk is that one can see defects in the woman before buying her – L's besotted lover cannot see the truth about the girl even when she is totally visible through her clothes). On *Coae vestes* see further Tibullus 2.4.29, Prop. 4.2.23. Hor.*Odes* 4.13.13.

1131-2 banquets: L is not indulging in anti-luxury moralising here for its own sake – though he elsewhere (5.1412-35) inveighs against the futile pursuit of pleasure through increased luxury – but is rather building up the catalogue of expense (note the asyndeton) to emphasise the waste, and the obsession; the lover spends everything but cannot enjoy it. On the real extent of anti-luxury sentiment among the Romans see Jenkyns 90-1 – not all Romans were Catos (cf Astin *Cato* 100-1), even if they sound like him (cf Williams 608-9).

1133 source: L may be thinking of the fountain of desire in Plato *Phaedrus* 255c, which flows from beloved to lover and back.

1134 bitterness: *amari* is clearly a play on words, reminding one of *amor* (love) – an 'equivocal word' (1137).

1136 sordid brothels: not all mistresses, of course, were

prostitutes – there was a whole range of amateurs and high-class *demi-mondaines* to pursue also. In all probability the beloved was less obtainable than a *scortum* (see J. Griffin (1981) 20), whose services were in no way inconsistent with Roman respectability (1065n: on the range of women see Lyne 8–17).

1137 shot: cf 1050–1n for the theme of the warfare of love; here, instead of Cupid firing love, we have the girl firing doubt and misery, a debunking of the romantic myth in a cynical scenario. ('The *real* arrows are...').

1140 laugh: cf 1125n, and notice the marked v alliteration.

1143 eyes shut: 'has the look of a colloquialism' (Bailey).

1145–50 Hunting metaphors, surprisingly uncommon in earlier poetry (see Kenney (1970) 386–8), except in the genre of the Hellenistic epigram (e.g. *AP* 5.64.4; 12.87.5–6). 'These "snares of love", familiar in the worthless poetry with which some of his readers must be presumed to be excessively familiar, really existed and were dangerous' (Kenney *art.cit.* 388).

1150 stand in your own way: a colloquialism. cf Otto *Sprichwörter* s.v. *obstare*.

1151–4 ignoring...blind: it is the refusal to see what is there which fetters the lover (*caeci* 1153). The first (*primum*) prerequisite for sanity is to look. This leads neatly into the *consolatio* theme of 'she's not worth it anyway'.

1155–6 foul..disgusting: *pravas* connotes deformity, mental and physical, coupled with *in deliciis* (sweethearts) in deliberate incongruity, just as *turpis* (disgraceful to be with, obscene) goes with *in honore*: the deformity is a darling, the slut is a queen.

1157–9 The proverbial irony of the beam and the mote, the besotted lovers offering each other wise advice on the idiocy of all loves but their own. *adflictentur* has the senses of sickness and also military harassment (*OLD* s.v. *afflicto* 1b, 2a).

1160–70 A famous catalogue. Sextus Empiricus' (*OP* 1.108) remark that 'many men who have ugly girlfriends think them highly attractive', used as evidence of the mode of differing circumstances in conditioning our evaluation of sense-evidence, is here transformed into a striking piece of satire, picking up an idea found in Plato (*Rep.* 474d). The fashionable Greek terms may be derived from Hellenistic love-epigrams, or may simply be the linguistic expression of the Hellenism that was rife in Rome (cf later Juv. 6.187–96).

1160 <u>honey-coloured</u>: cf Theocritus 10.26. *acosmos* is transliterated Greek.

1161 <u>image of Pallas</u>: Pallas Athene is often termed *glaukopis* (grey-green eyed) in Homer. *Palladium* is the word for a statue of the goddess.

1162 <u>one of the Graces</u>: *chariton mia* is again transliterated Greek. The phrase does not correspond to anything in Plato's list, and may be drawn from Callimachus *Ep*.51.1-2, (as suggested by Brown (1982) 89) or a later imitation (e.g. Meleager *AP* 5.149.2). On *merum sal* cf Catullus 86.4.

1165 <u>'livewire'</u>: *Lampadium* only occurs here, and is a diminutive form of *lampas* (Greek for 'lantern').

1168 <u>Ceres...Iacchus</u>: Iacchus is Bacchus, otherwise known as Liber; Cicero *De natura deorum* 2.34.62 declares that he was born of Ceres.

1169 <u>faun..Satyr</u>: cf 580n. *philema* is again transliterated Greek for 'kiss'.

1171-6 L continues the attack with exaggerated and gross descriptions of the girl – the poet seems to be as irrational in his despisal of her as the lover is in his adoration – couched in the styles of the *consolatio* (cf 1173-6n) and the diatribe, with its twin weapons of parody and quasi-realistic cynicism; the 'locked-out lover' (*exclusus amator*) is parodied, and the exterior superficial charms of the woman are deflated by the revelation of the 'reality'.

1171-2 <u>respectable her face</u>: the phrases *oris honore* – an assonance too musical for any but the most infatuated lover to use – and *cui Veneris membris vis omnibus exoriatur* ('power of Venus streams out of every limb') are surely parody of the fond lover's descriptions of his beloved – cf Catullus 86.5-6.

1173-6 <u>there are still...</u>: the three points of the *consolatio* for unrequited love are brought out by the tricolon crescendo, each phrase in the triad emphasised by the anaphora of *nempe*; the second point (we lived without her before) is similar to the point made in the great diatribe against the fear of death (3.832-7; see Wallach) that we were not miserable about being dead last time – before we were born. The third point – she isn't worth it – is stock sour grapes reasoning, but neatly positioned to lead into the extended satire of the woman and her lover.

1175-6 <u>disgusting smells</u>: Housman, in a learned note couched in the decent obscurity of a learned tongue (434) suggests that the only foul smells which would fit the context of maids sniggering and disillusioned lover are the girl's flatulence. This is vicious satire – but then L means it to be – and mild compared with e.g. Hor.*Epode* 8.

1177–9 locked-out lover: the figure of the *exclusus amator*, familiar from later love-elegy (Prop.1.16.17–44, Tib.1.2, Ovid *Amores* 1.6; see also Hor.*Odes* 1.25 (with Nisbet and Hubbard *ad loc*), 3.10) and satirised at Horace *Epode* 11. (cf Copley passim). The present passage surely puts the existence of such *exclusi amatores* beyond doubt – even though his description is a caricature, his satire would have no point if it did not allude to a recognisable phenomenon. Notice the variation in L's description; three different words for doors or parts of doorways (*limina... postes... foribus*), and three sets of actions: *covering* with flowers and garlands, *smearing* with marjoram (where the specificity of marjoram lends immediacy to the picture) and finally *implanting* kisses on the door. The cartoon-like mood is enhanced by the transferred epithet of *superbos* set against *miser* in the next line – the woodwork is snooty while the lover grovels outside.

1180 let him in: the MSS read *iam missum*, which is clearly corrupt. The most plausible emendation is Lambinus' *iam ammissum*, where the '-am am-' could easily have been merged by a scribe prone to haplography. Lachmann objected to the two participles together and proposed *ammissu*: but the rapid succession of participles adds a cinematographic swiftness and immediacy to the lover's entry and immediate disgust which are worth keeping.

1182 fall to bits: the short dissyllable *caaat* is poised and effective in the middle of the pompous *meditata diu... alte sumpta querella*; for all the time he has spent on it, for all the deep sincerity of his lament, he, drops it in the space of two short syllables. *querella* is parody of the lover's affectations – it is used at 548 of the plaintive song of birds.

1184 credit...mortal: *mortali concedere* is precisely what L recommends at 1191 *humanis concedere rebus*.

1185 goddesses of love: the use of *Venus* to ımean 'mistress' is paralleled in Horace (*Odes* 1.27.14; 33.13) and Vergil (*Ecl.*3.68). It remains an unusual, arch expression, however, ideal for the infatuated lover (as in Vergil) or the ironic commentator (Horace and L.). Just how divine they are is hinted at in 'back-stage realities'.

1186 back-stage: *postscaenia* occurs only here, and fits very well with L's other theatrical allusions (74-83, 768-772, 788-93). The point that the women are merely actresses, the lovers willingly suspending disbelief, is made with the utmost economy. As in the theatre, the illusion remains only until one looks behind the scenery.

1189 light: cf 8n. The romantic lover's illusions are a form of superstition (regarding women as goddesses, etc) which it is L's purpose to drag into the light of *ratio* (reason) (cf 1.146-8). 'Giggling' must refer back to the giggling of 1176, unless it means simply 'all this ridiculous state of affairs' as Robin suggests.

1190-1 kind-hearted: the colloquial *bello* is in deliberate contrast to the high-flown language of the lover; the man of common sense sees the girl as she is, in everyday language, unlike the romantic who dresses her obvious faults in pretentious euphemisms (1160-70). From this point on L gives positive advice on marital happiness in a manner shocking only to those who see him as a psychotic misogynist.

1192-1208 Having exposed the delusions of lovers, L now begins to treat of the realities of sex and reproduction. The haughty mistress affects not to desire sex - to raise her market-value - but L assures us that women genuinely enjoy the activity. The comparison with animals is an integral part of the argument, resting not on a despisal of women but on the realisation that 'people and animals function according to the same processes of nature' (Betensky 293; for an exceptionally sensitive treatment of L's use of animals see Amory 161-7).

1192 always: an ironic reference back to the 'goddesses of love' who deny their favours. Aristophanes liked to portray women as insatiably randy - cf *Lysistrata, Thesmophoriazusai* 383-519 - a judgement underlined by the interesting fragment 275 MW of Hesiod.

1193 body with..body: verbal coupling of the word; cf 1056, 1246.

1195 sincerely...mutual: her desire is for reciprocal pleasure; cf Aristophanes *Lys*.163, and Ovid's strictures on pederasty for this reason (*Ars Am* 2.683-4).

1196 race of love: cf 2.962, 3.1042, Ovid *Ars Am* 2.725-32. Adams (184-5) sees *sollicitat* as referring to 'unspecified acts of stimulation... during intercourse' (cf Ovid *Amores* 3.7.74).

1198 could: the subjunctive *possent*, followed by several verbs in the indicative, was disturbing enough to prompt Lachmann's emendation *possunt* – but as Bailey argues, the sequence is natural: 'they would not be able... but as a matter of fact'. cf 5.211-12.

1199 also: Brieger's *quoque* makes better sense than OQ *quod*, in the context: the female also, not just the male, overflows... *subat* picks up *subsidere*, and the eager asyndeton of *subat ardet* is emphasised by the assonance of *-at ardet abundans*.

1200 thrusting against: 'L is punning here, the woman's withdrawal is connected with the desire to *feel again* (*re-tractare*) the man's thrust.' (Fitzgerald 81 n.22). This is far preferable to Bailey's absurd 'with reluctant joy', which would make nonsense of *laeta*. For *Venus* meaning 'penis' cf Martial 3.75.6, Juv.11.167. *salio* has a range of meanings including: to leap, to ejaculate fluid, and to mount animals – an appropriate word to use here (cf *OLD* s.v. *salio* 1,3,4).

1202 bound...tortured: paradox here that the animals are tortured in mutual pleasure; for the image cf 1113.

1203 crossroads: the graphic location suggests primarily that the animals are pulling in opposite directions.

1207 trap: this would suggest that the joys they anticipate will disappoint – but the whole point is that their joys are real and mutual. The 'trap' is merely the post-coital lock.

1209-26 Heredity is through the seed, the child resembling the parent with the strongest seed, with even grandparents' seeds on occasion showing through. This view was largely traditional, being drawn from Democritus and the Atomists and also from the medical writers (Hippocrates *De genit.*7.8) and the Stoics (Aetius.5.11.3).

1210 overpower: the battle of the genders is well evoked by the strident *vim vicit..vi*, the two uses of *vis* locked together in verbal combat; cf *matrum materno... patribus patrio* for the same device used to recreate the origin of mother's-children in mother's seeds, etc.

1211 mother's seed: Epicurus believed that the woman also secretes seed in intercourse, L appearing to reason that if only fathers had seed, then all children would resemble their fathers. The problem is picked up again at 1227.

166

1215 goads: cf 1082n. The battle of the seeds is enacted within the clash of the bodies, but the apparent conflict (*obvia conflixit*) turns into a mutual conspiracy (*conspirans* playing on the sense of *spirans* 'breathing' – cf 1109).

1222: fathers...fathers: L telescopes the passage of time for the sake of the argument and to create a pleasing paradox – new-born babies are not yet fathers themselves.
'root of the race': *stirpe* is an archaic-sounding word, common in early Latin (e.g. Ennius *Ann* 178). Its use here suggests the long sequence of generations from the distant past.

1223-5 lottery...specific: the contrast in this passage is of the apparently random lottery of heredity and the scientifically determined process which is really at work; if our characteristics, right down to the fine detail of face, voice and hair, are produced 'from a specific seed', then it follows that in fact there is no more 'chance' of having a child with red hair than there is of giving birth to a sheep – if the atomic determinants are such and such. We must accordingly read *minus* (Lambinus' correction for *magis* OQ).

1227-32 Daughters resembling fathers and sons mothers proves that the determinant of gender is not the same as the determinant of appearance – in other words, sons are not made by the father's seed, daughters by the mother's, as might be supposed. Hippocrates noted this (*de genit.*7-8) and concluded that each sex has both male and female seed, the child needing both.

1227-8 female...father's: notice the interweaving of epithets in *muliebre* becoming *materno* crossed with *patrio* becoming *mares*, the juxtaposition of opposite sexes in each case recreating the mingling of disparate elements.

1230 more than an equal: L harks back to his statement (1209-17) that resemblance is brought about by superior strength of one seed over the other – he is not saying that gender is so determined, of course.

1232 scion...birth: *suboles* is cited as an archaism by Cicero *de orat.* 3.153, and suggests the traditional male heir to carry on the family. *origo* on the other hand suggests descent, birth (*OLD* s.v. *origo* 4a), again implying the future bearer of children.

1233-77 Sterility. Our inability to predict when sex will produce childbirth has often led to the supposition of magic or religious forces at work. L thus attempts, at this terminal part of the book, to demolish once again superstitious fears and fantasies, replacing them with sound - if crude - physical principles, substituting science for sorcery.

1233 divine powers: cf Homer *Iliad* 9.453-7, where old Phoinix ascribes his infertility to his father's curse calling on the Furies of the Underworld to render him sterile. For the denial of divine agency in human life cf 2.177-81, 5.195-9, 6.379-422.

1234-5 delightful: L sentimentalises the picture of infertility, as he sentimentalised family life at 3.894-9, to suggest the emotional indignation of those unfairly 'cursed' in this way. As he will explain, it is all a matter of science, which is only hindered by the infertile man's maudlin lament leading to absurd superstitious practices (1236-9).

1236-8 gods: L again satirises superstition: cf 1.84-101, 2.352-4, 414-7; 3.51-4; 6.68-79. The focus of the satire here is the ludicrous picture of them 'miserably' throwing vast quantities of blood onto altars, seeking to alleviate their pathetic virility anxiety (suggested in 'heavy with vast amounts of seed' (1238)).

1239 power: L plays off *numen* against *semen* - it is *semen*, not *numen*, which is needed.
sacred lots: for the famous Lots at Praeneste, feared by the emperor Tiberius and brought to Rome, cf Suetonius *Tiberius* 63.1, Cic.*de div.* 2.86, Prop. 2.32.3.

1240-62 L develops the interesting theory that fertility depends on a harmonious match of 'thick' and 'runny' seed.

1240-1 some..then again: note the variation of *nimium - praeter iustum*, and *partim - vicissim*.

1242 parts: for the coy *locis* see 1034n.

1245 fly forward: the repeated *pro-* sound emphasises the (futile) leap of the seed. On *ictu* cf 1273, Adams 145-9.

1246 seed..seed: for the verbal coupling cf 1193n.

1249-50 fill up...burden: cf 1275.

1251-3 previous marriages: serial polygamy was notoriously common among the Romans, at least among the upper classes (see examples in Lyne 5-6), and the *Laus Turiae* inscription makes it plain that infertility was a common enough reason for divorce (cf Friedländer vol.1 243) since childless men were under a disability in inheritance.

1253-6 rich..shore up..old age: for the notion of children as an investment for the future cf Euripides *Medea* 1033, *Alcestis* 633, Homer *Iliad* 24.540.

1259 thick..watery: notice the chiastic arrangement of the line: *crassa¹ ...liquidis² ..liquida² crassis¹*. West ((1969) 119) suggests that the varying quantity of the first syllable of *liquidus* is here onomatopoeic for the mingling of opposites.

1260-2 nourishment: diet was not mentioned as important in Hippocrates' treatise on the Seed (*de genit*), although he covers most of the other areas mentioned by L.

1263-77 Sexual position is also important in fertility, L asserts; and the fertility is in inverse proportion to the pleasure of sex.

1264-7 wild animals: the position envisaged is clearly rear-entry with the woman kneeling: 'this rather impersonal stance tends to be more gratifying to the man than to the woman' opines Johns (133), which may explain why 'wives don't move' (1268). The comparison with wild animals is not intended to be pejorative (cf 1192-1208n).

1268 our wives: this is not a snide jeer at the frigidity of wives – simply the observation that wives generally want children (see 1251-3n) and so do not need to employ the erotic movements which would inhibit conception. (But cf Martial 11.104.11 for a complaint over a wife who doesn't 'move', and see Adams 194).

1269 woman: wives, *qua* wives, do not move – but women *qua* women do.

1270 delight..thrusts away: exactly like the animals (1200n).

1271 body: Clausen (415) points out the difficulty of the MSS *pectore*: 'a woman undulates not with her whole breast but with her whole body...'. The text and meaning of *ciet fluctus* are both secure, and the stress on *clunibus* (buttocks) makes the *fluctus* extend right down the torso, not just making her whole breast limp – whatever that may mean – but her whole body.

1272 furrow: for the agricultural metaphor cf 1107, Adams 24-5, 82-3.

1276 at the same time: the prostitute kills two birds with one stone by both avoiding pregnancy and gratifying her customer.

1277 wives: cf 1268n.

1278-87 L closes the book with a gentle eulogy of marriage as honest friendship – in contrast to the deluded infatuation of the lover. Women were admitted to Epicurus' Garden, and were 'not excluded from friendship, the most important path to happiness' (Müller, *Fondations Hardt; Entretiens* 24 (1977) 214).

1278 <u>divine intervention:</u> cf 1233n. The reference to the 'arrows of Venus' is heavily sarcastic.

1279 <u>girl:</u> *muliercula* ('little woman') is often used patronisingly; cf Livy 34.7.7, Cic *Off.* 2.57 ('children and *mulierculae* may like the games, but a man...'). L's intention here is to build up to the surprise of *ametur* (she's ugly.. in shape.. the little woman.. but she's *loved*).

1281-2 <u>sees to it:</u> from the passives of 1279 we suddenly see the woman burst into action (*facit ipsa suis*) all by her own efforts.

1283 <u>intimacy:</u> the phrase sounds like a proverb – *concinnat* picks up *concinnior* from 1276.

1283-7 A final reminder that human beings are a part of the natural world, bound by the same laws; far from debasing people to the status of objects, this declares L's vision of the underlying unity of all things, the recognition of which is the only recipe for happiness.

1284 <u>frequent blows:</u> Otto (s.v. *creber*) compares the Greek proverb 'with many blows is the oak subdued'.

1286-7 <u>drops of water:</u> for the physical truth of this see 1.311-9, for its proverbial currency see Otto s.v. *gutta*, 2. The phrase is eloquently put here, with the verbal clashing of *guttas in saxa*. Minadeo (36 + n.5) suggests that this is 'an ironic twist of phallic wit', comparing Catullus 32.11 – although in this case it is the woman who is penetrating the man.